British and American Culture:

Evolution and Revolution

Fourth Edition

British and American Culture:
Evolution and Revolution

Fourth Edition

1판 1쇄 2018년 2월 23일
4판 2쇄 2024년 3월 15일
지은이 Jeremy Lawrence Sullivan
발행인 이진숙 펴낸곳 충남대학교출판문화원 주소 대전광역시 유성구 대학로 99
전화 042-821-6045 홈페이지 www.cnupress.co.kr E-mail cnupress@cnu.ac.kr

ISBN 979-11-6503-210-4 93740
정가 17,000원

British and American Culture:
Evolution and Revolution

Fourth Edition

Jeremy Lawrence Sullivan

충남대학교출판문화원

Dedications

For Howard and Frances Sullivan,

This book is especially for my mother; who nurtured and encouraged my nascent interest in language, read to me as a child, raised me to be an avid reader, saved my first pieces of writing and never discouraged me from being a Lit. Major despite the limited job prospects! And to my wife for her support during the writing process itself. It was a nearly impossible task in such a short time frame, but completely impossible without you. Thank you for your support.

Acknowledgements

Students in cultural studies often say to me that they dislike or even hate history, to which I respond , “then you must dislike every subject and discipline?” History includes all of what came before us and it informs everything in our memory our society, who and what we are. Without history human knowledge would never progress. That being said, it is understandable that students who are taught to memorize dates, statistics, facts, events, people’s names and time periods become exhausted. This cultural studies book is meant to emphasize the perspective and understanding we can gain by studying history from how it was understood at the time to the perspectives throughout the ages up until the present, as well as the constant revision and evolution of understanding that goes along with new contemporary discoveries about our past. This is where the book will start, before the beginning of recorded history where human culture can only be understood through scientific methods, technology archaeological findings and theory. This may seem irrelevant to the person trying to understand 21st century British or American culture, but exposing the roots in the environment, in the fundamental aspects of geography and in cultural inheritance remain surprisingly strong even though they are sometimes hidden from view. The chapters in this book will describe and analyze and connect revolutionary and evolutionary links in events and periods with the intention of constructing a is web-like picture of British and American culture that spirals outward. It will contain great gaps and intervals as it spins into being, but following the strands of cultural events, both sudden and short; gradual and long term, a clear coherent whole will be produced. Knowing the specifics of each of the events described in this book requires more in depth studyon narrower topics. So keep that in mind as you read through this book: that it is meant to be a springboard into more intense, specialized study of these cultures, but hopefully this will give the reader the fundamental building blocks and background that students need to progress in their understanding of these cultures and to support future endeavors in cultural studies.

I was heavily influenced by many historians, authors and even professional podcasters in preparing the material for the pages that follow. Just a few of the dedicated writers, speakers and researchers that I relied on for facts, quotes, perspectives and in depth description during the writing process are Robert Tombs, Howard Zinn, Jared Diamond, Dan Carlin, Mike Duncan, Christopher Bigsby, Simon Schama, Larry Schweikart, Lacey Baldwin Smith and Michael Allen. Any one of these scholars and any number of the books that are referenced in this work, some of them quite liberally, are highly recommended to the reader and you can find their work referenced in the bibliography at the end of this text.

A special thanks to the English department, the faculty of Humanities and the CNU CORE organization's grant, and in particular Dr. Sungshim Hong who was both the Dean of Humanities and the CORE Project leader of this program at the time this was written. She gave me the opportunity to publish this book and trusted in my ability and professionalism. Thank you to my colleagues who gave me assistance and advice and to my family for their support. And to all my students past, present and future that pick up this book to learn and develop your knowledge of culture, I hope you find it stimulating and comprehensive, you are the inspiration and my motivation for taking on this project in writing this book.

Prologue

How can one define what culture is? The task becomes simple if you choose to say, 'everything is culture.' Human life, humanity, ideas and experience all contribute to what we consider to be culture. The real difficulty we have in understanding culture lies in choosing what part of culture we study. Of all the available signs, what should we use as examples? What should we emphasize and examine? This is the quintessential question and the main challenged of a condensed work that attempts to cover as broad and complex a subject as "British and American culture." As William Shakespeare might say (or write) "ay, there's the rub."[1]

Thus, inevitably, with the constraints of time and space, I have made very difficult choices in selecting events, people and places to represent British and American culture. For the most part, as this is a book meant to be used for an introductory course for people that did not grow up in the United Kingdom or the United States themselves, I

1 Hamlet, William Shakespeare, Act III. Scene i. Line 65.

have followed the traditional and conventional examples. What I do hope, is that the perspective and analysis of those events is less biased and provides contemporary progressive views alongside what has been taught and understood in the past.

I have chosen to link the great and pivotal events of these two cultures, which once were one and are now seemingly forever separated, by their processes of change; whether they be slow or quick. Thus the title: 'Evolution and Revolution.' Following the definition of revolution given by the Encyclopedia Britannica we can understand a momentous event, such as the French Revolution as one that fits the main criteria of violence, speed and change. Whereas, even though an event like the Industrial Revolution might be of even greater significance, it occurs over a much longer period, has less significant outbursts of violence, but at the same time a more fundamental change and more human suffering overall. I have ventured to label these longer, broader, but deeper cultural events as 'evolutions' rather than 'revolutions.' Accepting that definition; events like the fall of the Roman Empire and the Black

Death, would fit much more comfortably into the former category, while normally being rejected by the latter.

What is Britain exactly and when did it come into existence? Is this simply an idea that we have retroactively applied in deference to the ancient Roman culture, to a thing that was never really wholly established, but just came into existence like a myth being assembled and constructed over time? That is a question that has recently been raised by revisionist historians as we uncover more and more of the buried, forgotten or hidden past. Before getting into a more detailed dissection of the culture of Britain, which along with the creation of an American culture, is what this book is primarily about, a quick definition of what the various terms mean may be of assistance as representative events, people, places and objects are laid out in this book. The introduction is designed to do just that: provide some context, terminology and basic theory for approaching the topics laid out chapter by chapter.

Will students in the future look back on this work of culture and judge it harshly for not being politically correct or for being narrow-minded, biased? Is this book too long-winded in some areas and too short in others? It is something that all writers of culture must guard against, but the limitations of time and experience will nonetheless expose this work as well, no matter how expertly the topics are navigated. Regardless, the effort to bring perspective, intimacy and depth to the quest for understanding each other must continue in literature and it is my fervent hope that this piece will convey to the reader the excitement and interest I have for this vast limitless subject! The wide scope of cultural studies should not discourage, but encourage us and if this book sparks the imagination and propels students forward to even greater thirst for knowledge of culture, then I consider it a success. So here it begins: the story of the evolutionary and revolutionary processes that produced British and American culture.

A short addition must be made here as this is the 4th iteration of the tome. Even until this past month had not expected to be working on this project for nearly a decade. I am pleased to observe that the material herein is just as relevant as in 2017. Certainly, the twenty-first century has advanced (if one may call it that) and technology continues to baffle. To the studious among you enjoy it critically and to the avid readers, I hope it is informative. My prologue, epilogue and dedications remain the same. Be entertained!

Contents

British and American Culture:
Evolution and Revolution

Introduction

Introduction

Cultural Studies: Britishness and Americanization

A casual passerby may, after picking up this book and glancing at its chapter headings, think that this is a history book. And while it is true that this book has been organized chronologically, and while it is chock full of historical content, it is primarily meant to inform the reader about the cultural development of two English speaking states: the United Kingdom of Great Britain and the United States of America. First and foremost it is concerned with the ups and downs, the progress and regress of these people and the historical narrative that it follows is meant to help form a cohesive whole that provides an overall understanding of British and American identity. So this is where it will start; with some clarification of what British and American terms mean and how they are used, followed by a short summary of common cultural studies terms that will be advantageous for people interested in understanding these cultures and other cultural perspectives.

Stone Henge is one of the most spectacular Neolithic structures remaining in the world. It is a designated a UNESCO world heritage site and is recognized as an ancient holy site used by the druidic orders of the Celtic tribes that occupied. England thousands of years ago. This precisely arranged astrologically accurate structure draws visitors from across the world wishing to catch a glimpse and feel the weight of eons of history and the signs of the original pagan religion of Britain's ancestors.

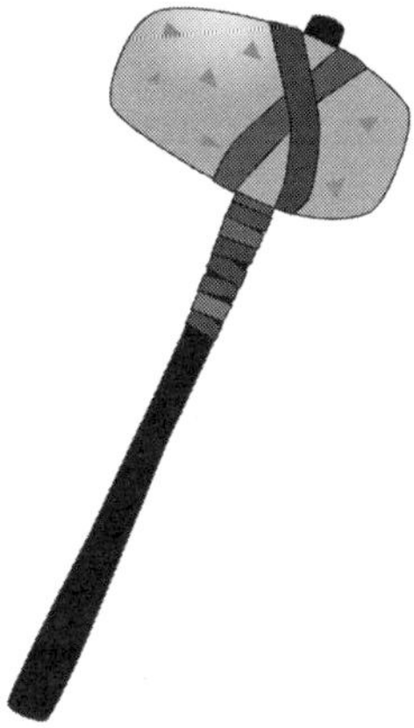

In the pre-Roman era the Celts had already started to use metal to fashion weapons and tools, but the original inhabitants of the British Isles did in fact live in the Stone Age. Clubs, flint and stone objects were used across the United Kingdom and remnants of them are still being found buried under layers of history.

A collage of common British symbols that have come to represent the United Kingdom across the globe (although they are primarily English and are focused around London and its history rather than the United Kingdom as a whole).

Great Britain

Starting with Britain itself seems logical if one is to derive the origin and meaning of "British." This is the most common and most modern of the terms currently in use, and refers both to the United Kingdom; in its present form, to the ancestral homeland of all the people within its borders and to the various forms it has taken from those prehistoric days up to the present. The most enduring and perhaps most significant of these labels was the British Empire, which mostly refers to the United Kingdom's 19th century global dominance, but was in use for several centuries as the signifier of British imperial power. The term Great Britain is meant to be both the present name for the nation state and a word that brings forth a long history, going back long before the term was actually coined and into a mythical British past. The tale of the origin of the British was reconstructed by its late renaissance imperial-aspiring culture and included the legendary figures of Robin Hood, Beowulf, King Arthur and many others. In fact, some went so far into the past that they claimed a connection to the royal bloodlines of the Trojans in Homer's Iliad. The pride in the fantastic (and fictional) accomplishments of the British people is implicit in their name "Great" Britain. It is linguistically derived from Latin when the Romans conquered the better part of the largest isle and occupied it for nearly four centuries evolving into Romano-Britons and giving it the name Britannia. British culture claims its inheritance from that first century A.D. Roman influence and the Celtic culture that preceded it, despite it being suppressed for many years under the weight of the people that followed it. Thus, Great Britain has attempted to unify this mixed and motley group of Britons, Romans, Anglo-Saxons, Danes and Normans, as well as Scots and Irish, under one umbrella, with a surprising degree of success.That success is one of the most important reasons that the state, despite recent calls for referendums and separation from the union in Scotland, persists as a culture.

This is what the evening view of the Thames and Westminster looks like in the present day. It features the Elizabeth Tower housing Big Ben and the Parliament buildings lit up by spotlights and lampposts.

However, people outside the United Kingdom have a tendency to misunderstand this projection of unity as homogeneity. There is an incredibly diverse and rich culture to be found in each part of the islands, each region and former kingdom, and even each city, town, village or hamlet. The dialects vary from county to county and shire to shire. This is why, on occasion, a North American with "British" ancestry may inadvertently offend an inhabitant of these isles who was not, in fact British. This is a faux pas that any person foreign to the isles may commit as the Irish live on the isles but do not identify as British. In fact, many Scots would prefer not to be referred to as British and they do not self-identify as one. Still more confusing to an outsider are the regional identities with their accompanying demonyms, such as; Londoner, Cornish, Mackem or Geordie. It is important to remember that this term has not been in regular use for much of recorded history and that it, like the term Great Britain has its political uses and terminology. This is not to be confused with the only slightly different spelling of "The British Islands" which refers only to the islands that are a part of the United Kingdom of Great Britain! In addition the British Islands include the Channel Islands, which are actually closer to the European continent than to the United Kingdom! After learning about these two almost identical terms and their widely different geographical and political meaning, it becomes easier to understand and to forgive the errors of the uninformed foreign observer. It should also be noted that, of course, the Scots, the Irish and the Welsh have their own terms for the archipelago, as do other nations, cultures and languages. Europeans have been known to call them the Atlantic Islands, but with the thousands of islands stretching from the west coast of Spain to the North America east coast, that term could be incredibly confusing, so it will not be used here.

The Britons

The people we now call the Britons are the people descended from the earliest inhabitants of the isles that we can confirm. Essentially the term refers to the mixture of Celtic tribes that occupied the land in the pre-Roman era. After the Romans departed the Celtic Briton culture briefly reasserted itself before succumbing to the horde of invading Germans, at least that is how the tale has been told. In order to illustrate a greater point about the understanding of British culture and its appropriation of history, an entertaining, but discriminatingly insightful comedy group will be called to the stage, as a the second source referenced in this book (after Shakespeare in the prologue): Monty Python.

Monty Python and the Holy Grail has long been considered, by those who grew up during the generation in which they produced their comedic masterpieces, to be one of the greatest historical film comedies of all time. It is consistently ranked among the top five comedies of all time of any movie genre, but whether or not you share that opinion of its lofty status or you tire of the endless references to its humorous scenes or you simply grew up after its time and have never heard of it Monty Python and the Holy Grail provides some of the most astute British satire out there. The following scene from that legendary film captures the essence of the never ending cultural conflict in British society between the upper class (represented by the traditional aristocracy in the form of the king here) and the commoner, while at the same time pointing to the regional indifference to the greater national unifying identity of being British (at the end of this scene Arthur ends up choking one of the peasants)!

The Britons, the ancestors of modern day Wales, who are now known as the Welsh, never called themselves that. Much like the Germans derive their name from the Latin term Germania, Western Civilisation is retroactively labeled all the tribes that occupied the Roman province the Britons. Recovering that ancient term, not just for the use of those ancient tribes, but for labeling the present day occupants of the territory south of Scotland (including Wales) was the work of a post medieval political effort to unify all the people occupying the British Isles under one 'British umbrella.' This made King Arthur, whether mythical or not, the common ancestor of all British people, and was part of that effort to forge a common identity. The following conversation is an excerpt from the transcript for the "Peasant Scene" in Monty Python and the Quest for the Holy Grail:

ARTHUR: How do you do, good lady. I am Arthur, King of the Britons. Whose castle is that?

WOMAN: King of the who?

ARTHUR: The Britons.

WOMAN: Who are the Britons?

ARTHUR: Well, we all are. We're all Britons and I am your king.

WOMAN: I didn't know we had a king. I thought we were an autonomous collective.

DENNIS: You're fooling yourself. We're living in a dictatorship. ..... A self-perpetuating autocracy in which the working classes--

WOMAN: Oh there you go, bringing class into it again.

DENNIS: That's what it's all about if only people would--

ARTHUR: Please, please good people. I am in haste. Who lives in that castle?

WOMAN: No one lives there.

ARTHUR: Then who is your lord?

WOMAN: We don't have a lord.

ARTHUR: What?[1]

The confusion over national identity here is classic. What would a peasant in a small village, labouring for his local lord (or in this case, for the community) know of national identity? The stark contrast between a life of daily toil for survival and a locally focused outlook in the Dark Ages with the public knowledge of national interests, international travel and global communication makes this scene all the more humorous. Is it possible to belong to a nation and not know it?

1 Gilliam, Terry, et al. Monty Python and the Holy Grail.

Was it possible to have a king lord over you and never catch a glimpse of him your entire life? Apparently, it was very possible and in many remote parts of the Isles, even probable.

This scene epitomizes the evolution of the British state and the constant clash of class interests that has been blamed on the Norman occupation dating from 1066, but has its origins going as far back as the Romans at the very least. Was ancient Britain free and wild, democratic and egalitarian? Hardly, but the concept of divine right, a synergy of the feudal structure and the hierarchy of the Christian Church, enabled kings to behave with a degree of impunity from at least the eleventh century. Arthur, though his actual existence is still unproven, represents an authoritarian figure here and not an enlightened one. The peasants can see through his façade and into the "violence inherent in the system" which enables rulers, whether good or bad, to dominant the population. In Medieval Britain[2] the king and a few men sat atop a vast pyramid with the teeming masses of poor serfs below. This on its own was enough in many instances over the course of British history to incite revolution in the short term and resistance that produced an evolution toward greater political representation over the long term. This is one of the main characteristics of British culture, especially in the past, and one that sets it apart from its European neighbors.

2 The terms "Medieval" and "Britain" are being used very loosely here. The age of King Arthus predated the Medieval period by centuries and the region he supposedly ruled over was only a part of southern England.

A view of the bridge crossing in front of Westminster Hall over the Thames from south London. The architecture itself is symbolic of British Imperial power and continues to wield the political authority it has since its inception. No such unifying symbol authority existed in the days of King Arthur of course! The legend of Camelot (if it ever existed) had to suffice.

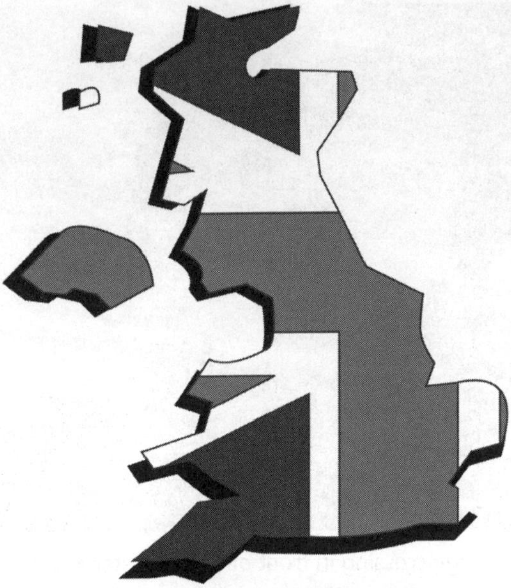

Even when viewing a rough contour map of the United Kingdom of Great Britain, one can see how it may have been divided. Once the elevations, tiny islands, bodies of water and precise coastlines are added, one can imagine how easily the land was divided amongst the ancient tribes that resided there.

This is the Star - Spangled Banner, the official flag of the United States of America, with its fifty stars representing the current number of states and thirteen alternation red and white stripes representing the original thirteen colonies of the union.

America

What, then, is an American?

The United States is the third most populous country, and it has the third largest land mass with the most arable land in the world.[3] In terms of sheer size and diversity it is unmatched in its geographical reach. Stretching from one ocean to the other, the width and breadth of a continent and with additional overseas states and territories it contains an amazing array of biodiversity across different climate zones. From Alaska, to Hawaii, Guam, New York, Texas, Florida and California, it is hard to put this nation in one box, let alone its culture. One could argue that it simply cannot be done. Besides there may be nothing wrong with not having a strong unifying homogeneous identity; just ask the current Prime Minister of Canada, Justin Trudeau whose 2017 federal government slogan read "Diversity is our Strength."

Nonetheless, for most Americans a strong sense of identity is an important thing to possess and is considered a definitive part of American character, by citizens and foreigners alike. With a strong reliance on stereotypes generated by the American dominated media, people normally do not have trouble imagining what an American looks like, how they behave, what they own and even what they think. This is a product of the global presence of America and the constant central spotlight it has occupied for the better part of a century in global affairs. However, being so ubiquitous has given this American

3 Nationmaster.http://www.nationmaster.com/country-info/stats/Agriculture/Arable-land/Hectares. January 1, 2018.

identity a polish and a Hollywood veneer that is hard to penetrate. It is as if the very fame that has made Americans so well-known even to the farthest corners of the world has also blinded them and the world to who they really are:

> In 2004, Bruce Springsteen, in explaining his reluctant decision to involve himself in that year's presidential election, remarked that in the aftermath of 9/11 "I felt the country's unity." He could not, though, "remember anything quite like it." Nor did the feeling last. The election, he suggested was essentially about "who we are, what we stand for," though what that "who" and "what" might be was clearly no more evident to him than those who had sung America a century and a half before, a Walt Whitman, say, who celebrated heterogeneity in what was offered as a national epic in which the narrative voice was an I that contained multitudes. "Why is it," Springsteen asked,
>
> That the wealthiest nation in the world finds it so hard to keep its promise and faith with its weakest citizens? Why do we continue to find it so difficult to see beyond the veil of race? How do we conduct ourselves during difficult times without killing the things we hold dear? Why does the fulfilment of our promise as a people always seem to be just within grasp yet for ever out of reach?
>
> He may have been "Born in the USA" but the question remained, what is this thing, the USA? That question has echoed down the corridors of American consciousness.[4]

It often seems as if there are more questions than answers when it

4 Christopher Bigsby. The Cambridge Companion to Modern American Culture. p.2

comes to American identity, but the same can be said of all nations and their multiculturalism. How does American culture engage with that diversity and attempt to navigate between its varying interests? The contradictions in American society are plentiful and that will become an important theme in the development of American culture through revolution, resistance, protest, evolution, war and peace. The very nature of America and the way it was born has compelled it to remain fragmentary and to struggle with itself. If anything an American identity is not fixed in place, but a thing based on freedom of expression and the right to occupy multiple identities at the same time. The most convincing proof of this is the heated, often explosive opposition that erupts when that freedom is threatened. The following chapters will demonstrate how American culture responds to attempts at curtailing its freedom, including when that threat comes from within.

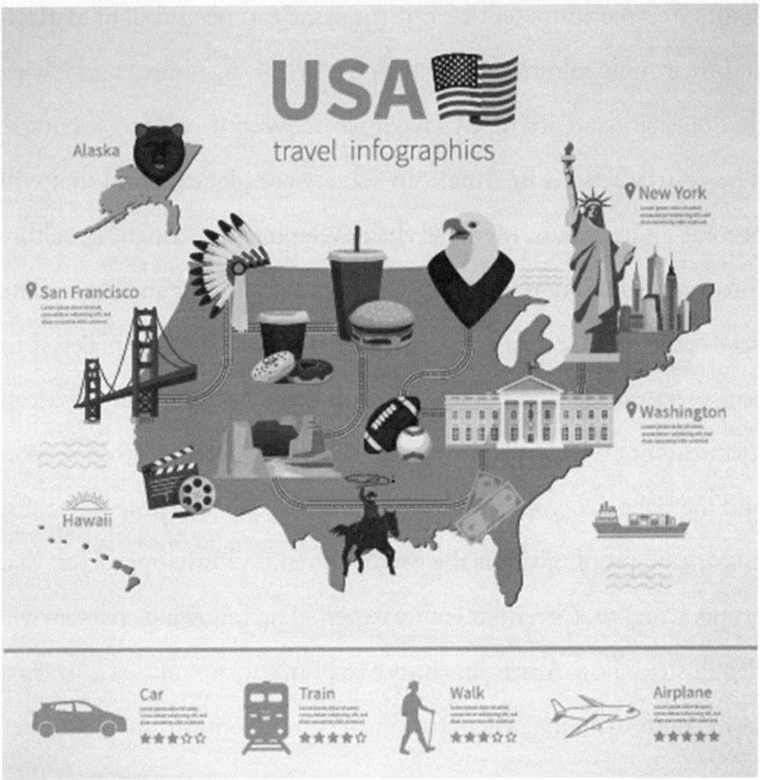

This simple infographic illustrates the stereotypes we use and the brands that we easily recognize around us every day. They often have their origins in the diverse interests that compose American culture. From food to sports to travel and architecture, the United States has exported its products, its media and its systems all over the world.

Regionalism

In the grand scheme of things the United States America is a very young country. Although it can lay claim to being the first modern democracy, its origins go back only a little farther than the latest chapter in the development of most Western states, let alone the

Eastern states. Its youth though has been seen in a mostly positive light, allowing it to start fresh, without the burden of history and long political and cultural entanglements. Another aspect related to its newness is the vast expanse of territory that lies within the American cultural sphere making it unique. The original colonies, founded by the English crown, companies, pilgrims and traders had a common cultural background, but the rapid spread of colonies to the south and west began to change this almost from the outset. This continued for a century and a half as the colonies of the English, French and Spanish grew mostly autonomously, but with the ebb and flow of war and peace on the European continent territories began to change hands, people were uprooted and cultural exchange occurred more and more often. Nothing was certain on the eve of the American Revolutionary War, not even the war itself. Many were opposed to it and the interests of the Continental Congress[5] did not match those of a variety of people across the thirteen colonies. Cultures began to emerge that were related to each region of North America, influenced by their geography, nationality, relations with native people, population density, economy and ethnic composition as immigrants from across Europe began to travel across the Atlantic and make a new home in America. In his introduction Colin Woodward divides North America into 11

5 The Continental Congress was the group of politicians representing the colonies' interests that met to decide the future of the British colonies in continental America, of which there were thirteen.

regional cultures and explains how they evolved and became distinct from each other:

> *American Nations* reveals the history of North America's nations from the moment of their respective foundations to their present positions within the continent's three federations: Canada, Mexico and the United States. It shows how their conflicting agendas shaped the scope and nature of the American Revolution, the Articles of Confederation, the Constitution, and a chain of violent citizen uprisings against the early American Republic. While every American knows about the great intraregional conflict that was the Civil War, it was in fact neither unprecedented (both Appalachia and New England entertained secession in the decades after the revolution) nor strictly two-sided. (The war actually involved a complicated six-nation diplomatic minuet over the future of the West). Northern Mexicans—including those who built the culture of what is now the extreme southwest of the United States—have for centuries seen themselves as separate from their purported countrymen in central and southern Mexico; they rallied behind numerous secession schemes, including the Texas Revolution of 1836. English-speaking Canadians endlessly ponder the weakness of their identity, and it's no wonder: their federation is comprised of very strong Québécois and far northern aboriginal entities and the northward extensions of four English-speaking regional nations whose cultural cores now lie in the United States.
>
> Disregard the conventional map of North America, with its depiction of a continent neatly divided into three federations, thirteen Canadian provinces and territories, thirty-one Mexican states, and fifty American ones. For the most part, those boundaries are as arbitrary as those chosen by European colonial powers to divide up the African continent. The lines on the map slash through cohesive cultures, creating massive cultural fissures in states like

> Maryland, Oregon, or New York, whose residents often found they have more in common with their neighbors in other states than they do with one another. Banish the meaningless "regions" with which we try to analyze national politics—"the Northeast," "the West" "the Midwest," or "the South"— whose boundaries are marked by those of their constituent states in complete disregard for the continent's actual settlement history and sectional rivalries. The continent's states, provinces, and federations do matter, of course, as they are official forums through which political power is exercised and expressed. But on carefully examining events of the past four centuries, one realizes these jurisdictions are illusions that mask the real forces that have always driven the affairs of our sprawling continent: the eleven stateless nations of North America.[6]

With the complexity of the confederation process in Canada, the American Revolutionary War and its consequences, as well as the Mexican Revolution, eleven sub cultures within the greater three nations may even seem like a low number, all things considered. Canada itself could easily be partitioned into five regions with their own cultural background, needs and identities, but that is beside the point. Far from being a melting pot of multiculturalism that produced a monocultural whole, the United States is rich in cultural diversity that has a long history of expression outside the official borders of nations and states. This too will be examined as the story of American cultural evolution unfolds in the subsequent chapters.

6 Colin Woodward. American Nations: A History of the Eleven Rival Regional Cultures of North America. p. 4-5

Cultural Studies

In this section, the use and application of Cultural Studies will be briefly outlined and discussed as this book is designed to introduce culture to students as much as it is designed for the population at large. This is useful because an analytical framework is very helpful in effectively examining, comparing or contrasting any aspect in the cultural field. To this end, Cultural Studies is a field of study that uses theory to conduct cultural analysis on society, history, traditions, conflicts and political interactions. Cultural theory is a useful tool for understanding the dynamics of cultural and for cross-cultural comparison.

Furthermore, in comparative cultural studies, we use the basic ideas of comparative literature alongside the approaches used in cultural studies to attempt an objective understanding of culture and cultural products. Literature, communication, media, art, events and even people are all examples of culture. Using cultural theories we can study culture from multiple perspectives to increase our knowledge of cultural interplay and effects.

- Through Cultural Studies we can attempt to be unbiased by using multiple biases. Multiple perspectives allow you to examine cultural contexts that go beyond your own culture. We use the word "attempt" because this method has its limitations as much as other theories do.
- We can break down cultural symbols and ideas into historical,

cultural and social contexts.

Social Context is used to analyze the world around the cultural phenomenon, whether it be an event, person, object or idea that is used to represent a culture. The word "milieu," which is derived from the French word for middle, is often used to describe a social context. There is also a term called "cultural milieu," but the social milieu provides a clearer definition and a connection to the environment and surroundings. In this context the representative cultural idea is physically somewhere and interacts with its surroundings. That is social context. For example, Abraham Lincoln or Queen Elizabeth II.

The picture above is a depiction of "Honest Abe," one of the most famous American Presidents. He was the President during a tumultuous period in American history, but successfully led the Union to victory in the Civil War before being assassinated by John Wilkes Booth while watching a performance.

Cultural context is more about ideology, traditions and values. The cultural milieu describes the relationship between these cultural forces and the symbol. These contexts are not limited to people only, many of them are objects or places. Good examples of this type of cultural symbol are the American Bald Eagle or an English breakfast.

Pictured here is a typical English style breakfast, featuring sausages, tomatoes, eggs, beans and tea. British food is often given little attention, and is seen as a bland simplistic when compared with the delicate and flavourful food of its French neighbours. However, order and cleanliness are rarely lacking in British dishes. All gastronomical factors aside, a central theme of British cuisine, it has been claimed, is functionality. So there you have it.

Historical context is connected to the events that occurred during the period the symbol existed, whether it be a person, place or object. It may, in fact, no longer exist in reality, but is still remembered as an important symbol with strong residual meaning. It is related to the "big picture" and takes into account national or international effects. A good example of this is any great historical event. Take, for example, the Battle of Quebec or the Invention of the Telephone.

The black and white photo above is of Alexander Graham Bell: A Scottish born, Canadian and American resident. He is claimed by all three peoples as their own because he is credited with inventing the telephone. For the purposes of this book, we will just call him "British."

Cultural Dynamics

Dominant Culture

A dominant culture is one that is the most powerful, popular or is the most important by effect in a region or sphere of influence. In social terms this can include the most common language, religion, set of values, art, ceremonies or customs. It does not matter how the culture is manifested, just that the representation has more influence than others of the same type. These aspects of the culture are normative and are the most visible signs of the culture. Cultural phenomena associated with this term are often referred to as mainstream, or even just as "pop" culture, although that term can be misleading.

Counterculture

A counterculture can be understood as resistant or deviant by mainstream culture because the values and behaviors exhibited by this group run against the grain of the dominant culture. Countercultures are rebellious, resistant and even revolutionary at their very core and thus are naturally opposed to (and by) dominant culture.

Sub-culture

A sub-culture has values and ideas that are not mainstream and it does not receive widespread support from the majority of the people in society. It is not resistant or deviant from the dominant culture in its region, but it has distinct features which it tries to maintain within its own space.

A breathtaking geographical satellite picture of the British Isles on a virtually cloudless day (a fairly uncommon event as an enduring British symbol is the umbrella as Rainy overcast skies are a marked meteorological feature).

The United Kingdom divided by counties and shires. When one thinks of regionalism the United States automatically comes to mind, but the cultural identity of the British Isles is even more specific and has a much longer history. In some areas it is said that it only requires a short walk and hopping a few fences to cross a county line, river or other geographical barrier to find a unique accent differing from the village or town that was left behind.

BR EXIT

The Royal Seal of Great Britain, pictured between the paper clips and underneath the declaration of EU membership. British culture has always been tied to the continent, especially to Germany and France, but at the same time due to their physical separation as an archipelago their need for autonomy, sovereignty and distinctiveness has been strongly pronounced. The obvious benefits to an economic and political union with the European continent have always been contentious in the United Kingdom and the referendum in 2016 where just over 50% of the citizens who voted expressed a desire to leave the European Union demonstrated how powerful that need for self-determination still is. The British passport remains one of the most powerful in the world and its traditional brand representated by its coat of arms will continue to carry a message of British pride and a long history of sovereign governmental management, no matter the outcome of the Brexit process.

The distinctive features of the Royal Seal of Great Britain is described below:

Above is a copy of the seal of Great Britain, a version of the British Royal Coat of Arms. The official coat of arms is only available with the express permission of her majesty the Queen, but a description of the full detail colour version is as follows:

[The] Royal Coat of Arms of the United Kingdom of Great Britain and Northern Ireland as used by Queen Elizabeth II from 1953 to the present (as used in all her realms except Scotland). " Quarterly, First and Fourth Gules three lions passant guardant in pale Or armed and langued Azure (for

England), Second quarter Or a lion rampant within a double tressureflory counter-flory Gules (for Scotland), Third quarter Azure a harp Or stringed Argent (for Ireland), the whole surrounded by the Garter; for a Crest, upon the Royal helm the imperial crown Proper, thereon a lion statant guardant Or imperially crowned Proper; Mantling Or and ermine; for Supporters, dexter a lion rampant guardant Or crowned as the Crest, sinister a unicorn Argent armed, crined and unguled Proper, gorged with a coronet Or composed of crosses patée and fleurs de lys a chain affixed thereto passing between the forelegs and reflexed over the back also Or; Motto 'Dieu et mon Droit' in the compartment below the shield, with the Union rose, shamrock and thistle engrafted on the same stem. " PINCHES, J.H & R.V., The Royal Heraldry of England, 1974, Heraldry (http://en.Wikipedia.org).

British and American Culture:
Evolution and Revolution

Chapter **01**

Britain, Britain, Britain

Chapter **01**

Britain, Britain, Britain

It is difficult to determine exactly where to start a history of a culture and a people. One could argue that Great Britain really did not truly begin until 1707, when the English and the Scottish agreed to be united politically, and even then unity has been a tenuous thing, as the Scottish Referendum in 2014 attested. However; I wish to include, as part of the description of British culture, the geography. The influence the terrain and location has had on the development of distinct culture in the British Isles is difficult to quantify, but whatever its exact effect, it certainly should not be excluded.

Starting with the first humans or proto-humans to ever arrive in the region is the logical absolute extreme end of the origin of culture argument. The very earliest humans to ever come to the area we now call Great Britain were a variety of homo- species that arrived as far back as 800,000 years ago! When modern human homo-sapiens split with Neanderthals approximately 600,000 years ago members of both species made their way across land-bridges that once connected the British Isles to the continent. Ice ages periodically wiped out settlements as humans were forced to take refuge farther south and then re-settle as the ice sheets receded. These cycles continued for over half a million years until the most recent cycle nearly 10,000 years ago ended with the warmer global temperatures we have now.

Fossil records, archeology and geography, among other fields and sciences have given us a wealth of new information about this prehistoric past, but perhaps the most reasonable place to start this discussion of culture, since we eventually want to arrive in the present, is at the end of the last ice age. Thus, we will make our way from prehistory towards a recorded history of the culture of these islands and beyond. The region began to be repopulated as people migrated across the shallow half-sunken region which is now fully submerged between England, Belgium, the Netherlands, northern France and the Baltic Sea; Doggerland. As the climate warmed and the polar ice retreated, water rushed in to fill the area scooped out by glaciers creating the cold and stormy North Sea. The retreating ice also left behind the rolling green hills and marshes of Ireland, the forested and hilly lands of England and the breathtakingly beautiful craggy rocks and lakes of what would one day be Scotland. These areas were gradually occupied by people hunting and gathering and resettling the continent. It has been estimated that the oldest ancestors of the British now inhabiting the Isles may have arrived as early as 15,000 year ago, but the earliest evidence of Neolithic culture dates from approximately 4000 B.C.E or 6000 years ago. This is when we can start to put together the first fragmentary pieces of a history of the British and their original cultural roots, many of which have long since disappeared, but some of which remain imprinted on the United Kingdom to this day.

There are dozens, if not hundreds of archaeological sites for tourists to peruse with interesting monuments and structures all across the British Isles from the Atlantic coast of Ireland to the south eastern cliffs of Dover to the farthest flung islands of the Hebrides at the northern most tip of Scotland. Usually the first thing that comes to mind when anyone mentions prehistoric Britain is of course, Stonehenge. However, before we discuss the unavoidable and influential henges of Britain, the equally fascinating Neolithic UNESCO World Heritage sites on Orkney Island are worth a closer look.

Celtic Britain: An Unwritten History

Although the dedicated Anglophile might prefer to have history commence with the coming of the Angles and the Saxons and their coinage and the name of Angleland—later corrupted to England—the Romans got there first and invented the term "Britain." The beginning of recorded British history started with Julius Caesar, because the Celtic population, who had arrived after 1000 BC to replace or intermingle with the original Bronze Age Beaker Folk and Urnfield People, had no written language and never recorded what they called their island home. However, Caesar's role in the Roman conquest was largely restricted to spreading the word that the island was ripe for the picking. He crossed the channel from Gaul in 55 BC and again in the following year, but was far too busy crossing his own Rubicon and limiting the number of would-be-emperors to one—himself—to worry about Celtic barbarians living a thousand miles from Rome and the center of politics and classical culture. Then, eleven years later on the Ides of March, he also was eliminated. As a consequence the serious conquest of the island did not begin until 43 AD when, eventually, a Romanizing force of 60,000 administrators and soldiers transformed some four to six million Celts into proper Roman citizens for the next 300 years. This was a "civilizing" feat matched only by the British themselves a millennium and a half later, when 160,000 Brits succeeded in anglicizing the 300 million inhabitants of the Indian subcontinent and making them proper subjects of the British Imperial Crown.[1]

Britannia

What was it like being under the Roman boot? It may not have been

1 Lacey Baldwin Smith.English History Made Brief, Irreverent, and Pleasurable. p. 7-8

as bad as some would assume. There is now evidence that many of the cooperative clans of Britain benefited from the Roman presence and occupied positions of authority in the local Roman government. The luxuries and products that came to the isle through the connections to the empire were a very attractive benefit to being compliant. Furthermore, the infrastructure that came with the Roman citizens that settled in the area provided trade benefits for all the residents of the British Isles. This is not to diminish the destruction and chaos that the Romans brought with them in "civilizing" the region, it is just to point out that later generations of Britons were Romanized and that many people were absorbed with persuasion, not coercion, into the empire. London was a cultural hub, the Rome of the north in its day and the citizens were a mixture of domestic blood and foreign culture; the Romano-Britons.

However, the Roman age was coming to a close at the end of the 4th century C.E. and an emergency recall of the British Legion turned into a permanent withdrawal and the natives were left to fend for themselves. Shortly after the departure of the military, the Roman magistrates were expelled, as the Romano-Britons attempted to re-organize their abandoned state to resist the raids of the Scots, Irish, Angles, Saxons and others.

The statue of Queen Boudica designed by Thomas Thornycroft next to the Parliament buildings in Westminster London, United Kingdom. This woman led a very dangerous revolt against the Roman overlords in Britannia, but the rebellion was doomed to failure and her forces were routed. The retribution was terrible and Boudica became the first of many heroic British female figures.

The Anglo-Saxons

King Alfred, the Great

Down through the ages, in all the glorious history of the British, there has only been two English kings deemed worthy along with Britain itself to be granted the title "Great" and the first is worth mentioning. Alfred was born the youngest of his father's sons in the kingdom of Wessex, which roughly corresponds to the modern day counties of Somerset, Dorset and Wiltshire. During his lifetime there were fierce and deadly Viking raids disrupting trade, production and life in general. After the death of his elder brother, he took command of the military forces in Wessex and succeeded in repelling the Vikings. After years of campaigning to free the countryside of the menacing barbarians he succeeded in making a truce and in recognizing the establishment of the Dane Law in northern England, which will be discussed shortly. He consolidated his kingdom and absorbed Essex on the way to becoming a confident and even-handed ruler. He encouraged the arts and literature and began taking stock of his kingdom, regulating taxation and military service so that both could be more effective. He established a code of laws entitle the "Doom book" which comes from the Anglo-Saxon word "Dome," meaning Law. He was a devout Christian and incorporated the laws of Moses into the laws of his kingdom. As a result of his efforts to reorganize his territory we have records and official letters that give us insight into the lives of the Anglo-Saxon people in the 9th century C.E. He was considered an enlightened leader for his day, and it is that reputation that earned him the epithet "the Great." Stories persist to this day of his unique personality and his upright behavior; the following story told by Lacey Baldwin Smith is an example:

> Legend has it that in 878, at the low point in his efforts to save his kingdom from destruction by the pagan Vikings, Alfred was forced into hiding and wandered with a small band of men "through the woods and fen fastnesses" of Somerset. Separated from his soldiers, he stumbled upon a swineherd's hut where in Christian charity he was given food and shelter for several days by a husband and wife who had no notion who he was. One day while Alfred sat in front of the fire, the wife began to bake bread, expecting him to keep an eye on the loaves. Deeply depressed and endeavoring to console and encourage himself by meditating upon the patience of Job in the face of divine affliction, and praying to St. Neot to intercede with God to save his kingdom from the pagans, the King forgot his culinary duties, failed to turn the loaves, and let them burn. The wife was justifiably outraged and scolded her careless guest: "You fail to turn the loaves which you see to be burning, yet you're quite happy to eat them when they come warm from the oven!" Duly chastised for his negligence, Alfred humbly directed his attention to the unkingly task of watching the bread. The story is not only a delightful homily on humility and self-control—Christian kings were not expected to go around fettering, blinding or mutilating each other or their subjects—it also raises the question of how St. Neot got into the story, since Roman Christianity was meant to have been destroyed

by the Anglo-Saxons and Heaven replaced by Valhalla.[2]

The legacy left by King Alfred the Great was one of exemplary leadership. In times of war, which were frequent, he was a brave, capable and dedicated military commander, and in times of peace, he was a reasonable and responsible statesman. His piety was self-evident, and although his merits have most likely been exaggerated over the centuries and his demerits minimized, his accomplishments and the tales of his model Christian behavior is memorialized in the minds of the people and the evolution of British culture.

Vikings, ho!

The Danelaw was a large portion of the area of modern day England covering most of the north and central area of the island. This area was colonized by invading Danish armies in the 9th century and would most likely have taken over the south as well, were it not for the aforementioned King Alfred. The Viking armies were composed of a mix of Scandanavians, but were dominated by their Danish leaders. As a result of their dominance of the northern seas and their spread across European coastlines, the people inhabiting the British Isles were largely helpless before their onslaught. Viking raids could appear and disappear suddenly, with little or no warning. The solution that Alfred came up

2 Lacey Baldwin Smith.English History Made Brief, Irreverent, and Pleasurable. P.13.

with involved militias and local forts, which enabled towns that were inland to repel the raids, but coastal towns, were largely at the mercy of the fierce invaders. The Danish laws were adopted in the area known as the Danelaw as a necessary compromise. The Anglo-Saxons were incapable of removing the Danish presence entirely and so they became content with a distinct Viking territory, which by the 11th century was merging with nearby kingdoms.

The entire northern central part of England was under the Danish influence for an extended period, but it was not all intensively settled or even directly affected by the Danish military aristocracy. Instead the Danelaw exerted a serious dominating cultural force that was backed up by the threat of force, which was manifested primarily through the courts and administrative system. The eastern coast was most affected by the Danish because of its proximity to Scandanavia, but areas farther inland were gradually affected too. The social, political and cultural ties became most pronounced as they reached peak in the form of King Cnut (Canute) the great who unified, in his own words,"... all England and Denmark and the Norwegians and some of the Swedes."[3]

3 M.K. Lawson. Cnut: England's Viking King.

This is a fascinating vestige of a building on Orkney Island in the Hebrides of northern Scotland. This is said to be the ruins of a Viking Church in Orphir. One can just imagine the tall imposing Vikings becoming solemn within its walls and observing a culture they had absorbed from the south tempering their desire to pillage and plunder the countryside, but after prayers for strength and forgiveness they likely returned to their longboats and set off down the coast of England to terrorize the coastal villages all the way to France!

Cnut the Great

The second of the two great kings in English history, was not actually English at all. Cnut the Great was born somewhere in the neighbourhood of 995 A.C.E. and was the son of Sweyn Forkbeard, an epic name for a king and father if there ever was one. He was the King of Denmark by inheritance, and also ruled England and Norway. The combination of countries he ruled is often referred to as the North Sea Empire and was almost unique in European history as he briefly brought the crowns of Denmark and England together. He was called Cnut the Great because he represented the pinnacle of Viking power after centuries of activity around the British Isles and the northern European coastline. He was well travelled and very active both on the sea and on land. His armies defeated Norway and Sweden in 1026 making him the virtual ruler of all the Viking kingdoms as well as the King of England. His dominion in England was largely unchallenged and stable, providing access to trade routes across the Viking territory from Iceland to Russia, and Norway to the Mediterranean. He actively promoted the integration of Danish and English culture which left a lasting mark despite its rapid decline in influence after his death. As the epithet "the Great" suggests, he was well liked by his Anglo-Saxon subjects as well as those in his homeland of Denmark. His image was tarnished somewhat by the subsequent Norman Conquest in their attempt to raise themselves up, by damaging the reputation of their predecessors, but Cnut's reputation as a fierce, but fair ruler of the north has endured despite their efforts.

Edward the Confessor

Edward the Confessor who was later known as Saint Edward the Confessor (after he was canonised by Pope Alexander III in 1161), was one of the last Anglo-Saxon monarchs to rule in England. Often people consider him to be the last true king of English descent, as his successor occupied the throne for less than a year. He was a direct descendant of Alfred the Great and the last king of the House of Wessex. His rule lasted from 1042 to 1066.

People have looked unfavorably at Edward's reign as leading to the disintegration of royal power in England and the simultaneous rise of the power of the House of Godwin. However, some biographers have described him as a successful monarch who was dedicated to his people and his country, even though he could be brutal and ruthless at times. Despite being portrayed as a listless, ineffectual monarch overshadowed by powerful nobles, Edward preserved much of the dignity of the crown and managed to keep the kingdom united during his reign of 24 years, which was a great accomplishment considering the power struggle going on between the Anglo-Saxons, the Danes, the Norwegians and the Normans. In the end though, his close ties to Normandy prepared the way for the conquest of England by the Normans in 1066. Some argue that it was the Norman Conquest and subsequent propaganda that led to his reputation being damaged until the Pope restored its lustre nearly a century later (Encyclopedia Britannica).

When he ascended the throne it was to succeed Cnut the Great's son, who was his half-brother, restoring the Anglo-Saxon line. However, he proved unable or unwilling to produce an heir which produced the dynastic crisis that led to the conquest of England. This type of crisis would become a repeated occurrence over English history as it has in other kingdoms, but none would be quite as catastrophic to the kingdom's English culture as the one following Edward's death. When he died in 1066 Harold Godwinson was given the crown, but he was immediately challenged from the north by his brother Tostig's alliance with the Norwegian king Harald Hadrada. Then, almost simultaneously, and as it turned out more importantly, his claim to the throne was contested from the south by Guillaume le bâtard (William the Bastard) Duke of Normandy, who is better known to history as William the Conqueror and William I of England.

Chapter **02**

Unsettling the Great Chain of Being

Chapter 02

Unsettling the Great Chain of Being

1066 – The Norman Invasion

It is not known exactly who coined the term "The Great Chain of Being," but it has its origins in the biological theories of the great Greek philosopher Aristotle. In his work entitled *History of Animals* he placed animals above plants due to their heightened ability to move, sense and feel. This eventually gave rise to an idea that both the Christian Church (the Catholic Church) and the aristocracy would latch onto: the idea of a great natural order created by God. They would use the Aristotelian logic, passages in the bible and the divinely ordained decrees of the Church to assert a social order that became the basis for the organisation of medieval life. All things from archangels in heaven to the lowliest creatures on earth had a place within this ranking which provided stability and security, especially for those born at the top of the chain. However, it is debatable how much this affected those who lived far from the king's court and the small urban centers, which was the majority of the population. Whether the average person living in England (Dane, Briton, Anglo-Saxon or otherwise) was affected by this concept or not, suddenly became a moot point as a great unsettling occurred with the Norman invasion. Soon the Norman occupation and domination of Anglo-Saxon-Danish England that followed their complete victory over King Harold at the battle of Hastings in 1066 would add a new people to the mix; the Normans. These people would dominate the top of the hierarchy as King William I of England doled out land and privileges to reward his knights. The results of the permanent Norman presence would be one of profound cultural and linguistic disruption, but little change in the hierarchical structure would take place as the Anglo-Saxon aristocracy was simply killed, replaced or displaced by their new Norman overlords.

Small fortified buildings enclosing courtyards and a keep became common across Europe and many remain standing in the United Kingdom to this day. Some have even become hotels for the historically or culturally curious tourist. Their original purpose; however, was not to entertain with dark, long drafty corridors and leaky stone walls, it was to defend against encroachment. The Normans were especially adept at building castles, and they did so in abundance across England and Wales to consolidate their power. These powerful symbols of medieval authority suppressed revolts amongst the peasants and ensured that local garrisons could hold out against uprisings and even invading armies until they could be relieved.

Centuries later Englishmen would continue to reference this period of Norman influence, beginning with William the Conqueror's victory over Harold at the Battle of Hastings as the "Norman Yoke," suggesting that people had been free beforehand and that the Normans had brought a new cruel elitist system with them that burdened the greater part of the population below. However, this revisionist version of history is simply not true and no matter how disruptive the invasion really was, it really amounted to a displacement of the Anglo-Saxon lords at the top of the social hierarchy and very little change at the bottom.[1] The lack of significant effect on the common people of England and especially on the Irish, Scottish and Welsh is evidenced by the continuation of their languages. Although French was imposed on the upper class by the Normans, and the first few kings, including William spoke French and could not speak a word of English, it would not take long for that to change. In less than a couple centuries French had completely died out and the aristocracy began to use English over French or even Latin (the official language of the Catholic Church) for all occasions including official business, diplomacy and in the courts, in addition to it already being the language of everyday communication. This period of foreign domination, which would end in the integration of the conquerors into English society would leave a lasting imprint on the English language, and therefore British culture. With respect to their national identity and its cultural memory, the British persistent paranoia of being invaded by another foreign power, in particular a Spanish or French invasion force, would soon be expressed by their obsession with northern France and the lowlands (modern day Belgium and the Netherlands).[2]

1 Some historians theorize that this is what occurred during the Roman era, but the evidence is less conclusive than that refuting the Norman Yoke theory, and so the debate continues.

2 For the past several centuries these key territories have also been referred to as "the Channel Ports."

Medieval Life and Times: Revolving Around Religion

Remember that to really understand what British culture was like in the Middle Ages, from the Norman Invasion to the Early Modern Period, you have to 'walk a mile in their shoes.' In other words, you have to imagine what it was like to live in a society where violence was prevalent and religion was the reason and explanation for everything. Society was organized into the great chain of being, where you stayed in your place as it was divinely pre-determined. God had made men kings and peasants, and that is where they belonged; it was natural and pre-ordained. Belief in God was widespread and expected. Christianity permeated society at all levels and was used by those in power to justify everything from political decisions to morals and education. Religion was also the explanation for how the world worked, as well as the science and philosophy of its day. The Roman Empire had been replaced by the institution of Catholicism and England and Scotland would continue to lean on it for guidance and legitimacy until Henry VIII severed that connection in the wake of the continental Protestant movement begun by Martin Luther. However, long before religion began to fragment and lay bare the contradictions and stresses in English and Scottish society during the Reformation, the Black Death would come along and upset everything for generations, including the ubiquity of religion and the stability of the unified European Christian church.

The Crusades

One important aspect of the centrality of religion to inhabitants of the British Isles, especially the kingdom of England, was its increasing militancy at the beginning of the second millennium. Christianity had been opposed to violence, as Jesus Christ himself was an advocate of peace. However, a cultural shift gained momentum as the warlike kings and nobles of Europe began to see themselves as soldiers of Christ. This transformation was slow, but when it was given the sanction of Pope Urban II in 1095, in gained frightening momentum as the warrior class across Europe answer the call to reclaim the Holy Land.

That religious war begun in 1095 is now referred to as "The Crusades" and it has always been controversial. The name itself was not in current use when the movement began in the late eleventh century, as in common parlance the expression was to "take up the cross," rather than to "go on crusade." This enormous movement of European people and resources toward the Middle East has had many important effects on Western culture as a whole, and as a significant kingdom involved in the effort to retake the Holy Land, the Kingdom of England, eas also profoundly affected. In fact, English culture would never be the same. Some signed up for redemption, some adventure, some glory, because of public pressure, opportunity, trade, to join a pilgrimage or any number of reasons! The journey was long and arduous, but the rewards were ever-lasting. And among all the English men and women that committed themselves to take up arms and challenge the Muslims for control of Jerusalem and its environs, the greatest was the eventual leader of the third crusade, King Richard the Lionheart.

In many ways Richard was the quintessential medieval king. He was a brave, handsome, skilled fighter; an intelligent and politically savvy leader; and a decisive, imposing, charismatic figure. He nurtured the arts, played at romance, was quick to anger, and to relent. He adhered strictly to the medieval hierarchy (the great chain of being), had a strong sense of honour and respected his opponents. He was a real life warrior-king who personally led his men into battle and funneled the vast resources of his kingdom into his war efforts. For two decades he fought bravely and gained a reputation as a fearsome knight. However, while on crusade he finally met his match on the field of battle when he fought the Muslim General Saladin the Great to a standstill along the coastal lands west of Jerusalem. His efforts bought the crusaders another 75 years or so in the Levant,[3] and access to Jerusalem for pilgrims, but inevitably the Europeans were expelled by the Muslim forces.

So this extraordinary event, beginning with Pope Urban II's call to take up the cross in the defense of the Holy Land in order to retake Jerusalem for Christianity, and ending with the fall of Acre, the last

3 The Levant is an old historical term that refers to the area now occupied by Syria, Lebanon, Jordan, Israel, Palestine and a small southern portion of Turkey.

Crusader stronghold in the Middle East, changed British culture forever. For nearly two centuries there was a firm connection between the British Isles, Italy, Turkey and the Levant. New products, goods, technologies, people, philosophies, languages and many other things were exchanged between people of various kingdoms, empires, religions and cultures. It is in these two centuries that one can truly see that the "Dark Ages" of the post Roman period in Western Europe had been overcome. Not since the Classical Roman period had such vast armies and the food, money, equipment, resources and manpower required to support them been assembled. It was a logistical feat on a different level, and despite the havoc wrecked by the Black Death, Medieval Britain as well as other European states, weathered the storm and were already testing the waters of the Atlantic as the Renaissance paved the way to the Early Modern Period.

The religious fervor, the participation in Church life, the shift toward sanctified violence as a part of the Christian ethos, are all significant cultural elements of the Crusader era. Churches were already the center of their communities, so with the cooperation of all levels of society the networking of the pan-European Church was able to encourage mass participation, if not cooperation. Donations poured in, holy orders multiplied and specialized, peasants and kings, soldiers and plowmen, young and old went on pilgrimages, traded, prayed, traveled and fought as they committed their lives to Christ. Not to say that all those that did so were honest, or that there were not cheaters, thieves, liars, hypocrites or miscreants, because there were many. Also, one must remember that from the perspective of the invaded, the Muslims, Armenians, Jews, Turks, Syrians and many others, the Crusaders were nothing but a group of violent, brutal, ravenous beasts. It was, in part, the resistance of the locals, along with the great strength and resources of a unified Muslim military that ended the Crusaders States, but this also coincided with reduced support and interest from the kingdoms of the West. For England, and for France, the Hundred Years' War was still in the distance, but the unifying effect of the Crusading effort had expired and tensions between European states flared up as they turned to fighting themselves. Thus, the 'us and them' division between Christianity and Islam subsided for a time, but has been constantly revived over the centuries since, reminding the Islamic world and the Europeans of their religiously motivated intrusion into the Middle East.

Power-sharing with the People

The Magna Carta was significant because it represented the first official attempt at limiting the powers of the King of England and forcing him to follow the law, rather than considering himself above it. However, its actual impact and significance in its own day is often overrated. It was centuries later during the English Civil War and in subsequent arguments about strengthening the role of Parliament in English society that the precedent the Magna Carta set began to have a great effect on the way the government functioned. It would influence the Glorious Revolution of 1688 and the American Revolutionary War and all the alterations of the British government to come, as well as the governments of its dominions up to the present. This, much more than its potency when it was signed, would be the lasting legacy of the "Great Charter" (which is its literal translation from Latin). For now though, in the year 1215 it would temporarily rein in King John, but do little more than that for the majority of the people who remained unrepresented. Of course the main benefactors of the documents were the Barons, who represented themselves as the landed aristocracy of the day and they would retain many of their newly reinforced rights. And, even though King John almost immediately rescinded on his commitments, the seeds of power sharing had been sown. It is true that kings would continue to rule by divine right for centuries, but little by little the system would evolve until more of the population had influence on the decisions and laws issued by the English (and then British) government.

The Trauma of Complete Devastation

The Black Death was devastating to Europe and the British Isles was no exception. The death toll may have been as high as 50% of the total population of the continent, but in some of the cities it was even higher than that. The plague was indiscriminate and left people, regardless of their class or status, dead wherever it went. The natural inclination of the population was to seek religious assistance, guidance, explanation and salvation. However, the Church was unable to provide these services and many people were left looking at a world without order. The great chain of being had become unhinged. Though this event was a disaster unparalleled in the history of western civilization it had some surprisingly positive consequences, for those that survived the apocalyptic disease. The sheer number of people that were left dead in the wake of the plague meant that labour was no longer cheap. In fact, human life itself was no longer cheap. Perhaps half the population of England died over five years, which crippled the economy, but made each man's contribution that much more valuable. Some scholars have theorized that this social upheaval and a questioning of the order of the universe was a huge factor in the development of Early Modern (Renaissance) society. Whether this is true or not, the immediate and long term cultural effects of the plague are undeniable as the population of England would not recover until the early 17th century, a period of over 250 years.

A Tumultuous Century

The 14th century was a time of fantastic change throughout Europe, and England was no exception. Famine struck the land and viruses killed off herds of cows and sheep, culminating in the Great Famine of 1315, while the climate became noticeably cooler causing repeated crop failures, diseases to spread and plagues continued to ravage the land. Populations were displaced, the class structure was upset and people began to seriously question their place in life. Of course in the midst of all this upheaval many incredibly influential people left their mark causing significant cultural change in both the short and long-term. Unfortunately, many of those contributions have not been recorded or were lost over time, so we cannot acknowledge many of the people, just their effects. As a result, only two of the most significant 14th century contemporaries will be briefly described here; the first, Geoffrey Chaucer (1343-1400) and the second, John Wycliffe (1330-1384). These two great historical figures had the most profound effect on the language and religion of England and their legacy was felt down through the centuries into the Reformation, the English Renaissance and beyond.

Geoffrey Chaucer

Other than William Shakespeare, there has been no more influential person on the English language than Geoffrey Chaucer. While most people consider the Bard of Avon to be the greatest English writer, the title of the Father of English should really go to Chaucer, who was the greatest Medieval writer. He layed the groundwork for all those who came after and would allow Shakespeare to claim "that all the world's a stage" whereas for Chaucer could only be a his stage was a smallish region of England. Chaucer grew up during the era of the Black Death, and he was well-connected to the upper class, but his chef d'oeuvre,[4]

4 Masterpiece or masterwork

The Canterbury Tales, provides us with a window into the life of Englishmen across the class spectrum in the Middle Ages. Though it is a work of fiction, its description, the lifelike quality of the characters, its portrayal of the social fabric underlying the behavior of the people and its revealing insights into the driving forces of 14th century culture make it unique. In his work he starts to form a written language from a combination of west Midlands English, Norman French and Latin. Drawing mostly from a spoken vernacular with huge gaps in its recorded written history and lacking a dictionary or common rules of spelling. So, one could argue that Chaucer was crafting a new language, at least in its written form. And indeed there were massive differences between Old English and the new Middle English that was coming into existence, making it more accessible, recognizable and familiar to English speakers of the time and of the twenty-first century. Beyond these contributions to the language itself, he also provided us with well-written and entertaining tales, poems and documents. Chaucer was also very influential in raising the status of the English language both domestically and abroad as he combined the vocabulary of three languages[5] with the Germanic structure of Old English, starting the consolidation process that would lead to all subsequent versions of English. Thus, he deserves the title "Father of English" and the credit for providing the basis for the language used by all the great poets, bards,

5 English, Latin and French

playwrights, songwriters, novelists and others of future generations.

John Wycliffe

The second of our two 14th century English cultural heroes, John Wycliffe, might justifiably be called the Father of the Reformation, or perhaps its Grandfather? Although he did not kick start the Reformation with a sudden and enduring revolutionary movement, and one cannot claim he had as much influence as Luther, he nonetheless could be called the theological father of English Protestantism. His ideas were advanced for his day and centered around the corruption of the Catholic Church, as well as the right of the common man to read the scriptures in the local vernacular. To that end he worked on translating the Bible into English. He was a scholar from Oxford and his ideas were grounded in reason and followed a humanistic vein. He insisted on rationalizing certain points of the Bible, and gaining a better understanding through interpretation. He gathered a sizable group of followers that were nicknamed "the Lollards,"[6] a term that was meant as an insult to their perspective on religion. Over the years the number of his followers waxed and then waned, but in many ways this early pro-Protestant group was the ancestor of very important social, political and religious groups, especially the Protestant denominations and they are well known to us because they were often referenced in political

6 Nearly a century later with the Catholic opposition to biblical translations the term would become equated with "heretic."

circles in later centuries.

The Consequences of the Black Death: The Peasants' Revolt of 1381

This Peasants' Revolt occurred because the social changes that had benefited the lower classes were being prevented by laws put forth by the King of England, at the insistence of the landed aristocracy. These restrictions and the taxes that were levied to support the Hundred Years' War being waged against the French crown on the continent triggered protest, then violence then a spectacular march on the capital and a confrontation with the King. The immediate result though, unfortunately for the peasants, was a rejection of their demands, armed reprisals and suppression of the resistance to the King's edicts. That is why this important event ends up as an evolutionary step, rather than a revolutionary leap. Wat Tyler's rebellion was snuffed out and the almost communistic demands of the peasants who rallied behind him were denied. Ultimately, though the conservative nature of the English allowed progress to be made and the freedom to work for flexible wages was permitted, as was the movement of the peasantry. The royal administration was wise enough to recognize the reality of the current conditions in an underpopulated countryside. Serfdom was abolished, the size and number of landholding peasantry grew. Thus the golden age of the yeomen farmer was born at the turn of the 14th century, meaning the 15th century became the golden age of labour.

A peasant's scythe was a simple tool that was normally an indispensable thing in the hands of a hard-working man. It was used for harvesting grain, but when necessary it could be used as a weapon. It also became the symbol of the Grim Reaper, a ghostly figure that was said to come when a soul was ready to be harvested and sent to the Afterlife. For centuries it also served as a symbol for the anger and discontent of the poor farmer at being suppressed and abused. As stated above, it was normally an agricultural tool, but in the absence of better equipment it could be taken up as a weapon.

Emerging English

Perhaps the most fundamental change in this time of changes was the sudden emergence of English as the first language of public life and modern literature. Since the Conquest, England had been the biggest multilingual and multicultural area in Western Europe, with educated people bi- or tri-lingual—"not three cultures, but one culture in three voices." Latin was the language of religion, scholarship and administration, and also (with a strong admixture of English and French words) of politics, business, law and everyday writing, even such things as household accounts. French, as well as having formal legal usage, was the language of fashionable culture. English remained as the everyday language, and also the language of religious piety. When it was useful, bits of the three languages were jumbled together.[7]

This may be hard for many people to imagine as English only began to emerge as the lingua franca at the turn of the nineteenth century at the insistence of the British Empire and then via American cultural hegemony. Nowadays, people in British and American culture have less pressure to learn a second or third language, and so they tend to be mono-lingual. Even before English became the global language of communication, nationalism had begun to impress one language on one people. The very possibility of the rise of English to prominence began, surprisingly, back in the fourteenth century when it became the official language used in the courts of England. And the rest, as they say, is history:

> Change came in an explosive burst, in hardly more than a lifetime, and it obliterated the remaining cultural divide dating from the Conquest. In 1362 law courts were ordered to use English. In 1363 Parliament was opened by the chancellor for the first time in English. From the 1380s parliamentary proceedings began to be recorded in English. In the "gramerscoles of Engelonde" children were abandoning French "and lurneþ an Englysch." Wills and guild records began to appear in English, and during the 1400s the records of manorial courts, customary rights and by-laws changed to English. There was an appetite for religious and secular literature in English, as a source for sermons, for private and public reading, and for

7 Robert Toombs. The English and Their History. p.129

performance.[8]

The English Unleashed

From the thirteenth century onward the English begin to dominate the British Isles, the nearby continental coast and their region in general on their way to becoming a unified first rate European power and a global empire. The Scottish Wars of Independence had established the Scottish as a sovereign nation once and for all, but the whole of England was unified and decidedly the stronger political, economic and military power, as well as being a vastly more populous kingdom. The Scots would periodically threaten the north, but would also never again be able to dispute English sovereignty despite great victories and political influence in the seventeenth century civil wars fought on English soil. The evolution from the devastation of the Black Death, through the Hundred Years' War, the War of the Roses and other conflicts, to the cultural heights of the English Renaissance in the sixteenth century. This series of great leaps, halting steps and stumbles, in which gradual and rapid change are interspersed propelling the English toward their eventual leadership in the formation of a greater British culture is described so concisely and eloquently by Robert Toombs in his introduction to part two of his historical text entitled The English and their History, that it

8 Robert Toombs. The English and Their History. p.129

deserves to be quoted in full here:

> The next three centuries saw the English unleashed: against their neighbours; from humiliating bonds of lordship; at times, against their monarchs; from the culture that had predominated since the Norman Conquest; against the Church; and against each other. Wars for the defence and conquest were fought on every land border, and across the sea in France, Flanders, Ireland and Spain. The subject status of villeinage... one of the targets of the 1381 Peasants' Revolt and a source of constant local resistance, largely disappeared, four centuries earlier than in most of Europe. Four kings were overthrown and killed, the nobility weakened, and ordinary people thrust their way into politics, claiming both ancient rights and a new voice. A modernized English language replaced French and Latin as the first language of politics, business, literature, law, even religion. The power and wealth of the Latin Church and its clergy were questioned. These upheavals coincided with—indeed, were connected with—devastating wars and social and economic catastrophe: population pressure, famine, plague and depopulation. Yet hardly, if ever, was the existence or unity of the nation, or the functioning of its institutions, seriously threatened. Despite everything, this was not a time of war of all against all. Revolts and civil wars aimed not to destroy but to restore what was believed to be the proper working of kingdom, Church and society. The worst civil violence was short, and the rule of law, however imperfect, was quickly restored.
>
> Some of this history is linked with European and global changes: famine and plague, due to volcanic eruptions and microbes. England became briefly a great European power, though later outdistanced by a resurgent France and the new power of the Habsburgs. Geography distanced it from the mighty confrontations between Islam and Christianity in the Mediterranean world, the economic and

> intellectual focus of Europe. Most of humanity was still fragmented by distance: great empires in China, India and Africa were shrouded in myth. Only at the very end of the period did Italians, Spanish and Portuguese begin the epoch-making contacts with east Asia and the western hemisphere. England, shaken by internal conflicts, by then had been left on the margins.[9]

The true extent to which the Black Death changed European society will never be accurately measured as the religious, social, political and even geographical chain reactions it set in motion were incredibly complex. Death on this scale had rarely been seen before and has never been seen since on the European continent. Even if all the great wars that have ravaged the people of Europe in years since are combined, they have not caused an equal amount of devestation. It was the medieval version of a nuclear holocaust. In fact, so many people died in the 1340s that entire areas were abandoned. The woodlands and thickets expanded and untended farmland was reclaimed by forests. The amount of agricultural land plummeted and production diminished. The death toll in England was such that it is estimated that the population did not recover from early 14th century levels until the 17th century. This means that four and a half centuries passed before English demographics and agricultural productivity were restored!

It was in this way that the plague caused a social revolution by increasing the wages, the value and the competitiveness of those who

9 Toombs, Robert. The English and Their History. p. 87-88.

remained. It also unsettled the class structure and the religious structure simply by wiping out an entire generation of well-trained, well-educated clergy. Ultimately though, the revolts would be put down and the status quo would be accepted again by many. Nevertheless European society had been rocked and the English in particular would evolve ever more quickly towards forcefully rearranging their society. Revolts, resistance and dissent were common and the political force of the people was slowly growing. A culture of individuality, of rights and of representation was taking root in the lands we would later call: British.

Marking the Modern Era

There are a number of different dates that are used to mark the beginning of the Early Modern period that vary widely from country to country, and rightly so. One of the most popular measures is the rediscovery of classical learning, the so-called Renaissance, or 'Rebirth,' that occurred in Italy first and then spread across the European continent, finally arriving in the British Isles a century later. Of course, this epoch defining change started as a trickle and quickly became a flood. As in other extended Revolutions, or if one prefers, 'evolutionary processes,' this approach is imprecise. In stark contrast to the slowly accelerating transformation of the Renaissance, we might mark the beginning of the Modern era with a particular date, such as 1453 with the simultaneous fall of Constantinople in the east to the Ottoman Turks and the final collapse of English forces in France, which effectively ended the Hundred Years' War. This is an exact date that has its own set of problems, but can be useful in determining when the European cultural shift became more apparent to the people at the time, as cultural change tended to be nearly imperceptible by those experiencing it, at least historically speaking. Of course, the subjective nature of using an exact date is also apparent. The date itself can easily be disputed. One might suggest that 1453 was too early, after all the English would retain possession of Calais for another century and would not renounce their claim to the French throne until 1800! This would seem to indicate that they English crown was hanging on to their Medieval past, in name if not in deed. Or, perhaps the end of the War of the Roses in 1485 when Henry VII, the founder of the Tudor dynasty, defeated Richard III in battle at Bosworth Field, ending the Yorkist faction's control of the monarchy is a better choice? A point in its favour is that this date would stand out during the English Reformation and the 16th century as a whole when the English began their imperialist ambitions by conquering and unifying the British Isles and then expanding overseas. This makes it an attractive choice, but it was cemented alongside 1453 in a similar manner by Shakespeare's history plays of which Richard III is one and Henry V another. Immortalized and romanticized, by later cultural shifts it is inevitable that there will never be a clear consensus on the matter, thus it is more beneficial to focus on the big picture of cultural change starting in the 14th century and continuing for hundreds of years afterward.

Chapter 03

Kings, Queens & Other Things

Chapter 03 Kings, Queens & Other Things

In many ways the sixteenth century is the most important of the eras in English history, in which the 'British' begin to rise again from being a regional power to a true global super power. It has even been suggested by some that a Tudor Revolution occurred, but this is a perspective that will not be adopted here. Nonetheless, it is true that there was a clear cultural change over the century that produced new ideas about Britishness. The British Isles had always had an influence on the affairs of the continent, even in Roman times, but now the other great states; France, Spain, Portugal, The Holy Roman Empire, the up and coming Russian Empire and even the empires in Asia would be forced to take notice of the British Isles as pivotal and central to the unfolding of world history. The increased geo-political power coincided with the flowering of English philosophy, arts, writing and other aspects of culture during the sixteenth century and would take off in the centuries to follow. Some would claim that the English language was unsuitable for law, politics, diplomacy or poetry, but Sir Thomas More, Sir Edmund Spenser, Sir Philip Sidney, Christopher Marlowe and of course William Shakespeare, would assure that English Literature took its place among the great mediums of human civilisation. In addition, by the end of Queen Elizabeth's reign the issue of religion would be largely settled, at least as far as Protestantism as a national religion was concerned and the process of "British" unification would begin with the two crowns being held by the same individual when King James VI of Scotland became King James I of England as well.

Religion also played a large role in the convergence of these two kingdoms as the Scottish Reformation occurred in parallel with the English Reformation. This would lead to the Scottish Enlightenment in particular, producing so many famous inventors, theologians, philosophers and thinkers. From there the unification of Great Britain would propel the new state into the Industrial Revolution. Despite all these positives, sixteenth century British Culture was characterized by tumultuous religious change and conflict, the authoritarian rule of Henry VIII and international conflict. Ultimately the succession of Queen Elizabeth in the mid-1500s would stabilize England, but things would remain tense at all levels of society. Going beyond the

Tudor Kings and Queens is essential though, as the age was marked by great men who contributed in many different fields. A last point of importance among the many great changes of the epoch defining century was the final linchpin in the empire-building effort, the construction of a navy as the British began to take control of the high seas.

Another Great Schism

On the eve of the Reformation, England was still a fiercely Catholic state, with its king, Henry VIII, being proclaimed Defender of the Faith for his campaigns on the continent against Protestant rebels. English, Scottish, Irish and Welsh life all revolved around the Christian Church and its power and authority stemmed from the Pope in Rome. This power was then disseminated through his ordained representatives the bishops and down through the hierarchy to the laypeople. England had two archbishops, in Canterbury and York, with the former having ex officio seniority. A long line of powerful men had occupied these positions and at times even challenged the authority of the king himself.[1] In England, as in other kingdoms and states, politics did not always align with religion, but the dedication and piety of the people was far too deep for any sort of systematic overhaul. However,

1 For example, Thomas Becket, Archbishop of Canterbury, who was slain by the knights of King Henry II for publicizing and criticizing the monarchy. He is often given the title of the 'first English celebrity' for his martyrdom.

after Martin Luther's ninety-five theses were posted on the doors of a German church and the bible had been translated into the vernacular languages of various regions, the ideological contagion began to spread like wildfire. Though the number of people converting in England was relatively small in the early sixteenth century, there was certainly a concerted effort to smuggle in and copy translated versions of the bible, which were quickly declared illegal by both the crown and Church. This policy did backfire to a degree when the English and Scottish Reformations got underway because there was already a nascent movement that included a dedicated minority that were willing to risk their lives to have access to the word of God, to read it and to worship in ways that ran counter to the instructions of the Roman Catholic Church.

The roots of the Reformation are deep and varied, so to understand the underpinnings of the Protestant Reformation it is important to first understand the Catholic system and what made multiple states rebel and reject it as the universal Christian Church. All the kingdoms of the British Isles were a part of this pan-European Catholic religious order at the outset of the sixteenth century. When the split occurred it was not as sudden as it seems in retrospect. Of course religious issues were at the center of the controversy, but each region had its own specific reasons for splitting with the Church in Rome, which in many cases went back centuries. So, before delving into the unique events that came to a head due to the political situation in the kingdoms of England, and of Scotland, as well as the impetus for their respective divorces with Catholicism; the political considerations of the English crown and personal gravity of Henry VIII, and the intensely Calvinist and bold Presbyterian movement in Scotland, let us examine the core ideas of both the Catholic Church on the one hand and the general principles behind the Protestant movement on the other.

The Core Ideas of Catholicism

Explaining and summarizing tenets of the Catholic faith is much easier than describing its Protestant counterpart because its very foundation is unity[2], but there is a surprising amount of diversity to be found in the 'Roman Catholic Church' as it is now called because it did spread all across Europe covering a dizzying array of people, cultures and languages while lasting for over a thousand years. It was able to do so by accommodating local and regional customs, by adapting to different cultures and by evolving to suit the needs of different people. When that evolution failed, and the hierarchy was no longer able to assert its will over the multicultural Catholic world, the northern European states broke away from its leadership one by one. To make the motivation for the break with the mother Church clearer, here is a basic simplified list of things that are part of the Catholic practice of worship, but were particularly disliked by Protestants who often

2 The word Catholic is derived from the Greek word "Katholikos" meaning "whole." This could also be translated as "entire" or "universal."

branded any of these ways of conducting worship as 'Popery.'

- A strict hierarchy with the Pope at its head
- Elaborate ceremonies, celebrations and festivals
- Decorative sanctuaries, ornate sculptures and stained glass windows
- The worship of Saints and the Virgin Mary
- The only bible permitted and available is in Latin translated from Greek
- The scriptures can only be interpreted by ordained clergy

The Catholic Church was, and still is, a strict hierarchy with local priests at the bottom and the Pope at its head. This structure was implemented during Christianity's initial spread and integration with the Roman Empire and has continued without interruption for nearly two millennia. Interestingly, the original Roman head of religion was the Pontificus Maximus; a position occupied by Julius Caesar among others, and is the reason why the Pope is still often referred to as the Pontiff.

The roots of the Roman Catholic Church are essential to its existence and its history can be traced to Jesus Christ and the Apostles. Over the course of centuries it has developed a highly sophisticated theology and an elaborate organizational structure that is headed by the papacy, the oldest continuing absolute monarchy in the world. The number of Roman Catholics in the world number close to 1.2 billion by some counts and there are more Roman Catholics than all other Christian groups put together.

Being one of the largest religions in the world, second only behind the Muslim faith, which is not unified to the same extent, Roman Catholicism is a very complex and diverse institution. When the Roman Empire fell, the Catholic Church gradually reclaimed the Empire's former European territories gradually absorbing and extending them even further to create a new hegemonic system. In some cases the only reason that Roman institutions and knowledge have been preserved over the centuries is because of the diligence of some in the Catholic Church. Over its existence it has endured multiple schisms, the rise of new sects and cults and endless theological disputes. It even survived the movement of its sacred capital from Rome to France and the simultaneous existence of three Popes!

Catholic England however was destined to fall, even though it had flourished for nine hundred years. After such a prolonged presence, it is not surprising that it left an indelible stamp on its English successor, the Anglican Church and its effect is still visible throughout British and American religions, as well as in other areas such as art, language, literature, law and architecture. Although its power and influence peaked in the Medieval period, it is nearly impossible to get a good grasp of Western culture without an understanding of Roman Catholicism.

The Core Ideas of Protestantism

The following points summarize the main ideas of Protestantism that will be emphasized in this book. There are a myriad of different denominations within Protestantism itself, which by its very nature began almost immediately to split again from Lutheranism and then again and again, resulting in many differing ways to worship and express Christian faith. These points are meant to broadly and generally encompass the main tenets of those denominations. Some fit to a greater or lesser extent, but only those within the British sphere will be discussed in this chapter in any detail.

- The Church is governed by a seminary headed by an elected moderator
- An emphasis is placed on simple worship services
- Sanctuaries are built to be plain and functional
- Worship of false idols is forbidden, as it is commanded in the Old testament
- Anyone is entitled to interpret the word of God for himself (woman were included much later)
- The bible is written in vernacular language (the commonly used language of the majority of the people in the region)

The Protestant movement began in northern Europe in the early sixteen century as a reaction to medieval Roman Catholic doctrines and practices. Along with Roman Catholicism and Eastern Orthodoxy, Protestantism became one of three major forces in Christianity. After a series of European religious wars in the sixteenth and seventeenth centuries, and especially in the nineteenth century, Protestantism began to spread throughout the world. Wherever Protestantism gained a foothold, it influenced the social, economic, political, and cultural life of the area.

The Origins of Protestantism

Protestantism in England would evolve in its own unique way because of the direct involvement of its king and because of its cultural and linguistic distinctiveness from continental Europe. It would include more radical elements, but for the most part the English Reformation would be more temperate and after some serious instability, persecution and violence, it would eventually pull back from radicalism and stay closer to traditional Catholic worship in settling on the moderate changes made in the Church of England. However, it is still necessary to understand the background of the broader Reformation in Europe as it did have a profound influence on England as well:

In the 16th century Protestant referred primarily to the two great schools of thought that arose in the Reformation, the Lutheran and the Reformed. In England in the early 17th century, the word was used to denote "orthodox" Protestants as opposed to those who were regarded by Anglicans as unorthodox, such as the Baptists or the Quakers.

Roman Catholics, however, used it for all who claimed to be Christian but opposed Catholicism (except the Eastern churches). They therefore included Baptists, Quakers, and Catholic-minded Anglicans under the term. Before the year 1700 this broad usage was accepted, though the word was not yet applied to Unitarians. The English Toleration Act of 1689 was titled "an Act for exempting their Majesties' Protestant subjects dissenting from the Church of England." But the act provided only for the toleration of the opinions known in England as "orthodox dissent" and conceded nothing to Unitarians. Throughout the 18th century the word Protestant was still defined in relation to the 16th-century Reformation (Encyclopedia Britannica).

Puritanism

These brands of English radical Protestantism stemmed from an attempt to reform and purify the Church of England to remove the last vestiges of Roman Catholicism. To them the religious settlements of Queen Elizabeth I were unsatisfactory and gave in too much to the Pope. Initially the name "Puritan" was used in a derogatory sense and the people practicing the belief did not self-identify as such, but the name eventually stuck. Their behavior was in stark contrast to their English Catholic and Anglican counterparts as they sought to reduce religious ceremony to its simplest form. Some critics of the movement defined Puritanism as "the fear that someone somewhere was having a good time" as their approach to worship was serious and somber. At one point during the English Commonwealth's brief existence they even went so far as to ban Christmas. Needless to say that policy failed spectacularly when the angry and/or drunken holiday-loving majority of the townsfolk spilled out onto the street Christmas morning and were told to go back to work!

Their efforts to convert society and enforce religious change were quite revolutionary for their day and were big factors in the outbreak of the English Civil War and the way life developed in the American colonies in the seventeenth century. In fact, many of the pilgrims were of the same Puritan stock that had tried to make the English Reformation even more extreme. A further more detailed, but concise definition follows here:

Puritanism may be defined primarily by the intensity of the religious experience that it fostered. Puritans believed that it was necessary to be in a covenant relationship with God in order to redeem one from one's sinful condition, that God had chosen to reveal salvation through preaching, and that the Holy Spirit was the energizing instrument of salvation. Calvinist theology and polity proved to be major influences in the formation of Puritan teachings. This naturally led to the rejection of much that was characteristic of Anglican ritual at the time, these being viewed as "popish idolatry." In its place the Puritans emphasized preaching that drew on images from scripture and from everyday experience. Still, because of the importance of preaching, the Puritans placed a premium on a learned ministry. The moral and religious earnestness that was characteristic of Puritans was combined with the doctrine of predestination inherited from Calvinism to produce a "covenant theology," a sense of themselves as elect spirits chosen by God to live godly lives both as individuals and as a community (Encyclopaedia Britannica).

A Puritan family following depicted in their home following a simple and strict lifestyle in the late sixteenth century England.

Sir Thomas More

One of the great figures to appear on the stage of history on the eve of the Reformation was Sir Thomas More (1478-1535), who takes his place amongst the heroes of this book for a slightly different reason than many of the others. It is his outstanding character, as much as his personal accomplishments that distinguish him as a unique Englishman. Of course he is well known for his literary contribution in writing Utopia, a satirical treatment of English society based on a fictitious island with suspicious similarities to his home country, but he was also a government official of high office (Lord Chancellor), a humanist social philosopher and an accomplished lawyer. He was a well-respected figure both domestically and abroad, earning the respect and admiration of many at court including King Henry VIII. Unfortunately, his loyalties lay on the wrong side of the Reformation and when it came to taking the oath of allegiance to the king, he flatly refused because of his devotion to the Catholic Church. His ideas have been adopted by thousands of intellectuals over the years for a variety of purposes, up to and including Catholicism, communism, socialism and humanism. His vision of a perfect state may not seem attractive to many of us, but his uncommon dedication to his family, his incredible loyalty and willingness to sacrifice himself showed his incredible strength of his will. After being pressured, interrogated and tried for his refusal to take the oath, he was executed by his former friend Henry the eighth even while he professed his loyalty to the king only after his loyalty to the Catholic Church. He became a martyr and eventually a saint, as well as a stoic example for the Catholic Counter Reformation both in England and abroad. A fascinating individual who will continue to stand the test of time as one of the most significant intellectual contributors to the English Renaissance who promoted humanism and human rights in

British Isles during the sixteenth century.

The Tudors

Henry VIII

King Henry (VIII) Tudor is one of the best known monarchs in English history. In fact, he is one of the best known monarchs in world history, and it is not because we celebrate his greatness, even though at times he was great. However, one's name does not go down in the annals of history when one is occasionally great; it gets memorialized when one is almost always great or a mercurial tyrannical manipulator. The man started a revolution ostensibly because he needed to divorce his wife, which was very politically insensitive to his Spanish Queen's country, Spain, and to the head of his religion, the Pope. That was a good start on the notorious side of the ledger! Then, after being excommunicated for divorcing Queen Catherine of Aragon anyway, he proceeded to marry and discard four more wives bringing his final tally to six. However, this revolving door of royal consorts is only part of the reason for his fame because it really was his forceful personality and the tumultuous times that he lived in, when unique and remarkable things were being accomplished, that put him in the permanent spotlight, all things considered.

The sixteenth century kicked off with a bang with explorers and adventurers by the dozens lining up to follow Columbus and Vasco de Gama, across the ocean to the New World and around the cape of Africa to the Orient. Close on the heels of that shift towards maritime exploration came the Reformation, which Henry became directly involved in by breaking with the Pope over the annulment of his marriage, as was just mentioned. He was a man of faith, spiritual and dedicated to God, which was normal in his day and age, but the dramatic spotlight he created for himself and his country was not. The international and personal drama that suddenly revolved around England had been absent since perhaps the Hundred Years' War, but Henry would start England on its path from side stage obscurity to dancing with the big players like France, Spain and the Holy Roman Empire. Someday England would be ranked highest among them and have its own special spotlight, this Henry must have thought, but that was not for some centuries yet. For now it was Henry's political and religious revolution that made England the first officially Protestant state with the Act of Supremacy in 1534 and brought such an intense glare to his corner of the continent. Robert Toombs gives a succinct description of the man here:

> Henry was conventionally pious, and unusually interested in scholarship and theology—quite capable of drawing his own conclusions and convincing himself of their rightness. He had fathered an illegitimate son in 1519—Henry Fitzroy, Duke of Richmond, who lived to adolescence—which convinced him that the problem was his marriage. It may in fact be that a genetic abnormality explains both his reproductive problems and his later

mental and physical decline; but his own diagnosis was that his marriage to Catherine was against God's commandments, as laid down in the book of Leviticus. His advisers produced a tailored translation of chapter 21, verse 20, supporting this conclusion: "Who so marrieth his brother's wife doth a thing that is unlawful, he shall be without sons or heirs male"—hence stillborn boys. (The literal meaning was "they shall be childless," which of course did not fit). He was, he decided, not validly married, and hence was free to marry again and produce an heir. At the opportune moment he fell passionately in love with Anne, the daughter of a friend and courtier, Sir Thomas Boleyn. She was vivacious and like the king interested in ideas. Although she was the sister of one of his earlier mistresses, they seem not to have become lovers: at first she resisted, and then he perhaps decided that, as future queen and mother of his heir, she must not become pregnant too soon. Frustrated desire certainly spurred what became Henry's obsession: to get rid of Catherine and marry Anne, an outcome for which he had to wait for over five years.[3]

The Elizabethan Age

Elizabeth I, the Virgin Queen, (born September 7, 1533, Greenwich, near London, England—died March 24, 1603, Richmond, Surrey), queen of England (1558–1603) during a period, when England asserted itself vigorously as a major European power in politics, commerce, and the arts (Encyclopedia Britannica).

Coming to the throne at the youthful age of 25, Elizabeth had spent much of her life locked in a tower wondering whether her fiercely

3 Robert Toombs. The English and Their History. p.164

Catholic older sister would have her permanently eliminated. She was also a near helpless prisoner and a victim of the advances of power hungry noblemen seeking political advantage through a relationship with her. Somehow she was able to ward them off and officially rebuff these men, while maintaining her dignity. She emerged relatively unscathed from the experience, although the traumatic experience of her first quarter century of life may have played a role in her decision not to ever marry.

Her success as a politician was almost immediate and her skill at court was obvious to all. She did not cause a revolution; rather she reversed some of the more radical elements of the English Reformation and chose the middle ground or the path of least resistance in most cases. This was one of her many talents, as she inspired her people with majestic royal displays and eloquent speeches. She continued the process of evolving England into a unified kingdom that her ancestors had begun. More territory began to fall under her sway, willingly or otherwise as she consolidated her hold on the home islands while expanding her power overseas through her endorsement of such legendary explorers and adventurers as Sir Francis Drake and Sir Walter Raleigh. Her impact was timely and pivotal, her influence grand and long-lasting. She was never given the title Great and she never produced an heir, but her importance is such that the entire period of English history is named after her. The latter half of the sixteenth century: the Elizabethan Age. Long live the Queen.

Since Queen Elizabeth had neither the power nor the money to build a substantial navy, especially while under the watchful and weary eyes of her neighbours in France, Spain and the Netherlands, she had to come up with an alternative plan. She ended up with a clever solution: why not let the enterprising sailors of the kingdom take it upon themselves to undertake the construction, manning, trading, maintenance and at times, protection of the ships themselves? She would provide some startup money in the form of loans and subsidies and when the "Privateers," so named because they were private and operated independently without government authority (except when she said, "protect Our Royal Majesty and Our Country), seized cargo or conducted trade. She would simply tax them and take a portion for the state and otherwise give them free rein. This brilliant and inexpensive tactic did build the English navy, but did not fool the Spanish in the least. Eventually they would tire of her coy games and innocent protestations that she was not involved and they would send a huge fleet of war galleons and soldiers called the 'Spanish Armada' in 1588. However, this terrifying large Catholic Spanish fleet sent by God to punish the Protestant English would get harassed by the English schooners and fireships, be unable to anchor and end up torn to shreds and shattered on the rocks of Ireland trying to make it home. Thus, the English received a sign of their destiny for greatness, both as God's chosen people and the lords of the sea.

The English Renaissance

And so, winding back the clock a half-century, to Elizabeth's youth, with the crown of England passing from Henry to his son Edward to Mary and finally to Elizabeth, where it settled until the end of the century. The strength of the Reformation had begun with Henry Tudor's Act of Supremacy in 1534, grown under Edward, but then reversed with his death when his sister Mary ascended the throne and began a Catholic counterrevolution persecuting people for practicing Protestant faith and burning them at the stake when they refused (or even if they did not in some cases) to recant. This earned her infamy and intense dislike of many an Englishman, as well as the moniker "Bloody" Mary. To this day, she remains one of the most unpopular English monarchs ever. Luckily, (for the Protestants at least) she took ill, supposedly with cancer of the womb, which was tragic for her because she initially thought she was pregnant, but when she passed away it was a relief for the Protestants, no matter their type because she was so fanatically Catholic. Thus, when Elizabeth was released from the tower of London and made Queen, most people were more than ready for her moderation, compromise and stability over persecution, violence and burning at the stake practiced by her elder half-sister. Elizabeth's settlements would provide the foundation for her long rule and for the Anglican Church itself, which has remained largely unchanged to this day.

So, the evolution of English religion stops there, officially, but unofficially the tensions between Catholics and Protestants remained and they were mixed up in the class tensions of the rich and poor at the same time. There were plenty of underground movements across the kingdom, as some people became closet Catholics and others wanted to become even more radically Protestant (Puritan or otherwise). The Scots dove headlong into Presbyterianism, but Catholics continued to lurk amongst them for the next century trying to maintain their international brotherhood, while Ireland simply remained staunchly Catholic for obvious cultural reasons (resisting English hegemony being the main one). On the surface with Queen Elizabeth ably steering the national ship, stability and unity returned and religious differences ceased to be a serious public issue. However, after her death and that of her nephew and successor James I, everything would boil over again triggering the English Civil War. But this is all still a half a century in the future as the inept Charles I has still not even been born yet. For now it is up to the humanists, the philosophers, the poets and the playwrights to carry the torch of religious fervor in the open. Putting theological arguments to verse and using clever devices such as allegory and satire, to avoid serious backlash, it was their responsibility to keep the spirit of the Reformation alive, or to reject it. During this period there were many who were attracted to English literature as Queen Elizabeth and her court were generous patrons of the arts. Some people sneered at the use of English as a literary tongue and some just wondered if it even had the capacity for poetic expression. However, any doubters would soon be overwhelmed with evidence as a certain man would undertake this project and lead it with an extraordinary amount of creativity and zeal. That man, was the great bard himself, William Shakespeare.

William Shakespeare

William Shakespeare also spelled Shakspere, byname Bard of Avon (baptized April 26, 1564, Stratford-upon-Avon, Warwickshire, England—died April 23, 1616, Stratford-upon-Avon), English poet, dramatist and actor, often called the English national poet and considered by many to be the greatest dramatist of all time (Encyclopedia Britannica).

It is hard to over-estimate the influence of this one man, as posterity has rarely been kinder to a playwright, poet or author. Whether the plethora of courses, art, memorials, honors or references is warranted or not, it is certainly arguable that no single British person has been more influential over the centuries:

England's greatest writer (1564-1616) appeared during its greatest revolution of words. The two are surely linked. That a man of outstanding intelligence should be stimulated to write by the political and cultural ferments of the time is easy to understand. But that a clever boy from Warwickshire should end up writing plays for the new London stage (the first public theatre was built in 1576), rather than works of theology in an Oxford college, is not so predictable. The professional theatre grew out of a widespread tradition of religious plays which from the 1530s onwards gradually fell victim to repression by the evangelical clergy, who considered them superstitious or blasphemous: God was not portrayed on stage in England between 1570 and 1951.[4]

Shakespeare was an innovator. He went far beyond Chaucer in linking English literature with contemporary European culture—an ambition that explains much of the brilliance of English literature at this time, even though many contemporaries doubted that England could produce a great literature because the language seemed to be changing so rapidly. Eventually Shakespeare's writing became central to the whole history of European culture, placing the English literature of these few decades on an equal footing with the classics. But this could only happen long after his death, because English remained practically unknown outside the islands until the late eighteenth century. Unlike More, and later Bacon and Newton, who wrote for an international readership in Latin, he was unread abroad for at least 150 years after his death, and it took as long again before he was considered as more than an exotic English primitive.

Like other English writers since Chaucer, he worked to stretch English into new forms for new uses—in his case, for all the genres of classical and Renaissance literature. So he was a great inventor of words—probably about 1,700, several times more than any other

4 Robert Toombs. The English and Their History. p.202

English writer at a time when word-making was at a peak. [5]

The Flowering of English Literature

In terms of everyday life, no piece of literature was more prolific or influential than the Bible. In the past Bibles were kept in private collections as precious works of art, and the English one word Common Book of Prayer did not exist. Hand-written manuscripts were prohibitively expensive for the average British person, but after Gutenberg the printing press had allowed mass production of the most important book in Western history to be reproduced in English.

> The Bible and the Prayer Book were the books that everyone heard, read and memorized—for many, the only books they possessed, a whole literature suddenly acquired and made universally available. Only Foxe's Book of Martyrs had comparable reach. A standard form of English became familiar across the country, without replacing spoken dialects. In France, in contrast, where most worship remained in Latin, French remained a foreign language in large parts of the country until well into the nineteenth century. This had an importance beyond the linguistic, though wetake it so much for granted that we overlook it. In countries from Wales to Ethiopia, where language, culture or statehood were inchoate or threatened a vernacular Bible and liturgy could preserve or even create a sense of national identity and a common culture. In England, where such identity already existed, the effect must have been powerfulas a constant reminder of belonging to what has been called the "imagined

5 Toombs, Robert. The English and Their History. p.203

community" of nationhood, now extended to all worshippers, men, women and children. As one historian has remarked with only slight hyperbole, for centuries to come it would be possible to check one's watch at 11:08 on a Sunday morning and know that at that moment everyone in the land was intoning the same psalm.[6]

The English Civil War

It always seems to come down to taxes at a certain point with revolutionary uprisings and in the mid 17th century when King Charles refused to work with the English parliament to pass legislation approving "fair" new taxes for government revenue streams a stalemate ensued. The resulting standoff came to a head when the King tried to use his authority to force the country to support him. England then divided into Royalists and Parliamentarians and fought across the entire British Isles into areas of England, Scotland and even Ireland. The King was eventually defeated, captured, tried and executed. Oliver Cromwell, Lord Protector of England was Charles' replacement and became king in all but name. However, this revolution was short-lived as after Cromwell's death the English monarchy was restored, but it was a monarchy with reduced power as the time of the English absolute monarch was over.

The importance of this event cannot be over-estimated as it centered on all the religious, political and social issues that had driven the English

6 Robert Toombs. The English and Their History. p.202

Reformation a century before. The English Civil War stopped short of being stamped the English Revolution because its new political structure reverted with the Restoration ten years afterward and the Glorious Revolution that opened the door to real constitutional monarchy. Thus it is overshadowed by its later French counterpart in 1789 (almost one hundred and fifty years later), even though the French too became a monarchy, then an empire and then reverted back to a Republic again. Regardless of whether its status as a true revolution is valid or not, the English Civil War marks a unique, though short, period in British history. It drove further religious reform, some of it radical, and increased England's maritime presence through trade and colonial expansion. Its contribution can be seen as a "Great Leap Forward" in the evolution of British culture. It formed military, religious, economic and political alliances that brought the kingdoms of England, Scotland and Ireland closer together and paved the way toward the union of England and Scotland thereby creating a new British state and cementing the modern British culture we know today. This unification along with continued maritime aggression would bring England and then Great Britain into conflict with its neighbours, namely: the Netherlands, France and Spain. This too was the legacy of the English Civil War and the short-lived Commonwealth as the British would continue unflaggingly to pursue their destiny to rule the waves.

The man mounted on the horse and immortalized in a statue at Trafalgar Square is none other than the controversial Oliver Cromwell, one time Lord Protector of the Commonwealth of England. His harsh subdual of Ireland and Scotland and his strict Puritanism (and his general anti-Catholicism) earned him notoriety along with fame.

The culmination of the English Revolution of culture, religion and politics would come in the form of a bitter and bloody fracturing of the kingdom during the English Civil War, but was followed several decades later by the Restoration then further stabilized with the Protestant led, but relatively conservative "Glorious Revolution" of

1688. However, it must be said that revolution in this case is a bit of a misnomer as what truly occurred was the re-establishment of a monarchy and a change to a dynasty that aligned with their cultural identity. This new monarch would not be an absolutist, but would wield greatly reduced executive power balanced by an even stronger parliament, all under the auspices of insistent English Protestantism and English nationalism (despite the fact that William of Orange was Dutch and that he brought a Dutch army with him)! The troubling reality of allowing a foreign army to invade and replace an English king with a foreign born prince was overlooked, as his firmly Protestant faith and matrimonial lineage relating him to the English royal bloodline was sufficient for the English, soon to be British, citizenry to embrace King William and expel the Catholic King James II, giving England its symbolic and popular national unity back again.

A Country Split in Twain

The aforementioned Magna Carta often gets credit for setting the wheels of democracy in motion all the way back in 1215, and in terms of an evolutionary movement in that direction, that point of view can be validated. But, if the Magna Carta provided the impetus, the fuel and set the kindling for the blaze, it was the outbreak of the English Civil War in 1642 that provided the spark that set the pile alight.

> The great divide of the sixteenth and seventeenth continues to shape our ideas of who and what we are. It has been enshrined in historical writing of unique importance, which more than any other historical narrative or political ideology shaped England's identity for at least two centuries, and still has echoes today. From the time of the Restoration onwards, royalist histories, memoirs, petitions and sermons defended Charles and attacked his enemies as power-hungry fanatics. Commonwealth histories, let off the leash by the 1688 revolution, dwelt on Stuart tyranny, Puritan sufferings, and Parliament's defence of ancient liberties.1 Each side had its dead heroes. On one side "King Charles the Martyr," celebrated by the Church on 30 January. On the other hand, John Hampden and Algernon Sidney: the "Good Old Cause" was long summed up as that for which "Hampden bled on the field and Sidney on the scaffold."[7]

It was also during this time that the Enlightenment began to take off. The insistence on public education in Scotland was paying dividends as literacy rates sky-rocketed. People naturally moved on from their enforced religious study of the bible to classical literature, philosophy and contemporary writing. This had a knock-on effect in England and the result was almost revolutionary in itself: the sudden appearance of an entire generation of innovative, scientific and creative thinkers in a relatively small population. Perhaps chief among them was the Scottish intellectual David Hume:

7 Robert Toombs. The English and Their History. p.264

David Hume, one of the greatest of the Scottish Enlightenment philosophers, used history as a powerful weapon against what he considered pernicious political myths. His history of England (1557) provided an accessible and "rapid" narrative for readers with only a six-volume attention span. His Scottish publishers, convinced that they had a best-seller on their hands, claimed that Hume was "truely imparshal." Some of the clergy condemned Hume as irreligious, not without reason; and he openly despised the religious quarrels of the Civil War period. He advised his readers that "extremes of all kind are to be avoided." His core idea was that societies progressed through stages of development by improving education, government, law and economic organization. Hume wanted to efface the dangerous Whig-Tory "party rage," which celebrated conflict and was not his view a basis for rational and peaceful politics. He went about this principally by demolishing every Whig shibboleth with grim relish. Saying that he would "hasten thro' the obscure and uninteresting period" of Anglo-Saxon England, he dismissed it as "extremely aristocratical," oppressive and violent. There was no "Norman Yoke": the Conquest had been beneficial, teaching the "rude" Saxons "the rudiments of science and cultivation." The medieval struggles of parliaments were the work of a "narrow aristocracy" and gave no benefit to the people; and Magna Carta brought "no innovation in the political or public law of the country." Anyway, freedom was not born in England: "Both the privileges of the peers and the liberty of the commons" were copied from France. As for the father of Paliament, Simon de Montfort, his "violence, ingratiatude, tyranny, rapacity and treachery" made his death "the most happy event which could have happened to the English nation." Thus Hume hoped to cut the umbilical cord connecting the English political imagination to an idealized past, which should be left in "silence and oblivion."[8]

This unresolved conflict of class, religion and politics was to spill over into other British territories one by one. The unrest could be seen at home, but it was easier for the establishment to rein it in on the home isles. Ireland experienced the downside of proximity to their imperial overlords again and again over the centuries as they never ceased resisting. As result many people would emigrate abroad for social and religious reasons, as much as economic ones. The vast distance to the overseas colonies would provide a space for burgeoning revolutionary movements to gather force:

> The English revolutions of the 17th century brought representative government and opened up discussions of democracy. But, as English historian Christopher Hill wrote in The Puritan Revolution: "The establishment of parliamentary supremacy, of the rule of law, no doubt mainly benefited the men of property." The kind of arbitrary taxation that threatened the security of property was overthrown, monopolies were ended to give more free reign to business, and sea power began to be used for an imperial policy abroad, including the conquest of Ireland. The levelers and diggers, two political movements which wanted to carry equality into the economics sphere, were put down by the Revolution.
>
> One can see the reality of Locke's nice phrases about representative government in the class divisions and conflicts in England and followed the Revolution that Locke supported. At the very time

8 Robert Toombs. The English and Their History. p.265

the American scene was becoming tense, in 1768, England was a racked by riots and strikes — of coal heavers, sawmill workers, hatters, weavers sailors — because of the high price of bread and the miserable wages. *The Annual Register* reviewed the events of the spring and summer of 1768:

A general dissatisfaction unhappily prevailed on several of the lower orders of the people. This hill temper, which is partly occasioned by the high price of provisions, and partly proceeded from other causes, too frequently manifested itself in acts of tumult and riot, Which were productive Of the most melancholy consequences.[9]

Most British did not see it coming, but another revolution was in the air. For now that the French had been defeated and had signed the Treaty of Paris in 1763, and Great Britain ruled North America unopposed. However, the stirrings and murmurings among its own people would soon prove to be a premonition of a new and even more critical internal struggle for supremacy in North America.

Intellectual Giants of the 17th Century

The Age of Enlightenment is said to have begun in the early 17th century. Across Europe there was a shift away from reliance on scripture and church officials, toward empirical knowledge, experimentation, logic and above all reason. The power of the human mind to investigate, test, discover and learn about the world became a curiosity that intellectuals could not resist. For English culture, this went hand-

9 Howard Zinn. A People's History of the United States p. 74

in-hand with the Protestant Reformation. Increased levels in literacy as a by-product of the printing press, the increasing availability of education to the public, the demand for better tools and technology, international trade, exploration and colonization, a financial revolution; among other factors, produced an environment that nurtured new ideas. The great poets Shakespeare, Milton, Spenser, Johnson and others experimented with ideas through literature, but it was in the 17th century that clearer visions of modern philosophy, nature and science began to emerge. And while there may be dozens of great people that contributed to this new process of enlightenment, only two exemplars will be presented here: John Locke and Isaac Newton.

John Locke

John Locke is significant because he is often seen as the father of liberalism. In a country such as England, where conservatism and tradition have been the order of the day for centuries, this philosopher's view stands out. Perhaps it is not surprising then, in a century that saw dramatic religious, political, financial and social change, that a man like John Locke emerged. His ideas were incredibly influential and affected many of the philosophers that followed, both at home in England and abroad. Fundamental to his ideas were his association of the self with consciousness. He saw a person as an impressionable individual open to being affected by the environment. He labeled this concept tabula rasa, which translates as blank slate. All individuals were born neither good, nor evil and it was the environment that made them so. He was a dedicated empiricist, which meant that he believed in experimentation and testing, so that when something was disproved and not repeatable, it was discarded. This is not dissimilar to the process of clinical trials that is used to screen modern medicine before they are approved for licensing and distribution. Locke was part of a generation of Europeans who:

For the first time since the decline of the Roman Empire… began to think about the universe without instinctively deferring to the superior wisdom of the ancient authorities, whether hallowed religious teachings, long-accepted philosophical and scientific principles, or immemorial laws, proverbs and customs. They were 'the first intellectuals on record to express an entirely secular awareness of social and economic changes in their society.'[10]

This new mode of thought was connected to the religious subjectivity that had destabilized the British Isles for over a century, but despite all these progressive and modern perspectives, Locke remained a staunch determinist, believing that the individual has no agency and that the world is pre-determined even as it was rooted in natural rights, order and equality.

10 Toombs, Robert. 279

Isaac Newton

Isaac Newton, the son of a farmer, was born in 1642, the very year the English Civil War began. From his humble beginnings he rose to become one of the greatest intellectuals of his age. He is still remembered in the legend of his own telling, as the man who; was inspired to harness the universe into a mathematical formula for gravity. He became a celebrity as his work elevated him above his contemporaries; a legendary figure in his own time. He was the first mathematician to be knighted, became the Chair of the Royal Society and his *Philosophiæ Naturalis Principia Mathematica* is considered one of the greatest intellectual works of all-time. It was "his fundamental insights into the forces holding the universe together [that] prevailed until the twentieth century, and are still used for many purposes"[11] today. The shadow he cast was so vast that further progress in logic and mathematics occurred abroad, rather than diverge from Newton's approaches. Culturally, he inspired whole generations and kingdoms of individuals to contemplate the universe. People who subscribed to his philosophy were, and still are, referred to as Newtonians. They believed that the world could be rationalized, that religion could also follow the natural principles and order in the physical world that Newton had discovered. Thus, his ideas were still anchored in the Anglican belief that science and religion could be reconciled and many English

11 Toombs, Robert. 280

supported that idea. The very idea that a man of science can also be a man of God may seem paradoxical to some in the twenty-first century, but Isaac Newton was such a man, and we would do well to remember the millions of British and Americans who, to this day, continue to cling to both science and religion despite the incongruity

Post-Reformation and Renaissance England and Scotland:

The Enlightenment (and the Union)

To return to the evolution of England and Scotland into a new unified state, we must discuss once more the consequences of Cromwell's commonwealth. One result of the unending shifts of religious and political groups and their fracturing, was a culture that was fatigued by infighting. Two centuries of inter-class and inter-religious warfare had left a population that still longed for unity. However, the conflicts of the British were mild compared to some nations and their maintainance of a functional kingdom and a stable society throughout it all, produced envy in some on the continent. Robert Toombs once again explains:

> Between the late 1600s and the early 1800s, the English, like their neighbours, collectively drew back aghast from the extremism and dogmatism—"enthusiasm," as they termed it—that disrupted life for two centuries. People in Europe learned to contemplate the universe and themselves in consciously new ways, entering what

> some called an "Age of Enlightenment" or "Age of Reason." Now other interests and ideas could be pursued, with more varied and less exclusive places to socialize, outside the church, inn and household. This stimulated new ways of getting and spending, which rewarded economic innovation, accelerated overseas contacts and conflicts, and eventually ignited a world-transforming technological and social revolution. Europe began its global ascendancy as the great Asian empires declined, and, more than ever before, contact with other parts of the world affected European life intellectually, economically and politically. England participated in these global changes, and eventually, for the first time in its history, led them.
>
> For intellectuals and politicians observing from neighbouring nations, all this made post-revolution England seem a very unusual country, inspiring admiration, envy and alarm.It had apparently achieved at a stroke open government, religious toleration and relative peace. As Voltaire put it, "The civil wars of ancient Rome brought slavery, but the troubles in England have brought liberty." Unexpectedly, this was also making it more efficient, powerful and wealthy, changing it rapidly from European laughing stock to global great power. For the first time, the English language and English ideas, arts and fashions spread far beyond its shores, even inspiring "Anglomania" across Europe.[12]

It was as if England was finally coming out of its shell, and being joined by Scotland at that. To become innovators and leaders in their own right. The Italians, Spanish and French had burst into the early modern age already and their renaissances were practically over, but

12 Robert Toombs. The English and Their History. p. 277-278

despite this late arrival the English and Scottish achieved similar cultural heights with even more rapid religious, political and economic changes. The rate of English, soon to be British, development would soon outpace all its neighbours eclipsing all of them by the nineteenth century. As a result of these momentous changes in the balance of power the English in particular have prized progress as one of the foundational ideas of the Enlightenment "...as utopian fantasies about the future came to rival fantasies about a past golden age as sources of political and moral inspiration. At this time, England and Europe came to believe that they had discovered (or rediscovered from the ancient world) universal ideas and values which they hoped the rest of humanity would one day accept. It is too early to say whether they were right."[13]

13 Robert Toombs. The English and Their History. p.278

The Scottish Part of the Union

The history of the Scots up until their King (James VI) unified the crowns of England and Scotland has largely been ignored thus far in this text, but this is not because Scottish culture was not visible, vibrant and influential. What follows is the briefest and most inadequate of summaries of this fascinating culture inherited by today's inhabitants of the United Kingdom of Great Britain.

The terrain of Scotland is notoriously rugged and had a tendency throughout history to produce or require similarly rugged individuals.

The Romans, English, Danish, Norwegians, Swedes and Normans all tried their hand at trying to subdue the Scots, but to no avail. The combination of geography, resilience and resourcefulness prevented the successful completion of any campaign to conquer the kingdom. So it was that in 1603, at the death of Queen Elizabeth, James VI of Scotland became simultaneously James I of England, founding the Stuart dynasty. Now, the fact that the 'hungry Scots' descended on London along with their liege lord did not endear them to their new brethren/hosts, but it also did not detracdt from the smooth, bloodless transition to a new monarch and the triumph of the Stuart accession. First James would leave an indelible impresson, commissioning the King James Bible, acting as European peacemaker, supporting and then siezing the fledlging Virginia Company and refusing to compromise of Church matters. However, the next Stuart his son Charles I would be far less capable, recklessly plungin his realms into multiple wars culminating in the English Civil War, which would conclude with his losing his obstinate and politically inept head. In the end he would die for his convictions that the monarch is ultimately soverign and after an interregnum presided over by the Puritans, Charles the Second was invited back in "The Restoration."

After further religious, political and military struggles Queen Ann would unite the two kingdoms creating the United Kingdom of Great Britain. Never since have they been separated and ever since the British has presided over a Constitutional

Monarchy that is one of the most democratic in the world Thus, the distinctive dress; the kilt, the musical instrument; the bagpipes, the language; Gaelic, the exotic food; haggis and many other things persist as uniquely Scottish elements of British culture. In fact, many Scots would claim their culture was never fully absorbed by the act of union in 1707 and that it remains a separate culture and it some ways it is.[14] Just ask the national Rugby or Football teams of Scotland!

Although it has remained a junior partner in this relationship, its craggy peaks and winding rivers would remain home to millions of Scots and to the summer homes of distinguished nobles such as Queen Victoria who summered at Balmoral Castle. It once constructed and housed the greatest naval fleet in the world at Scapa Flow and is rich in natural resources. Furthermore, it is often enough that England is the one that plays admirer to the unique culture and character of the Scots, whose participation in the union has been less of a fusion and more of an effective collaboration over the last three centureies. A visit to this part of Britain is to be transported in time and place, as well as to escape the increasingly uncomfortably hot summers.

14 This is evidenced by the narrow margin of the "No" don't leave vote in the 2017 Scottish Referendum.

Chapter **04**

The Hard Fork

Chapter 04 The Hard Fork

The Age of Rediscovery

British culture would, of course, be permanently split, but this was by no means a foregone conclusion, especially in the mid eighteenth century. All the stars had to align to give America its freedom and to forge a new destiny. To understand how and why this momentous schism of British culture occurred, requires going right back to the chronological beginning of chapter two to the confluence of Norse and Anglo-Saxon culture during the late Dark Ages and into the early Middle Ages.

The first confirmed intrepid European explorers to visit and settle in the Americas were in fact the Norsemen during the Age of

Vikings," which roughly coincides with the era of Alfred and Cnut discussed in chapter one. By island hopping across the Atlantic starting in approximately 800 C.E. with the Faeroes Islands North West of Scotland and arriving at Labrador and Newfoundland two hundred years later in approximately 1000 C.E. in what is now modern day Canada, the Norse planted colonies of small villages which archaeologists have uncovered for us to examine across the north Atlantic. Scientists are confident that they are in fact Norse settlements because of the resemblance of construction and design to Viking sites in the United Kingdom, Iceland and Scandanavia. However, these settlements were not to last and were abandoned no more than a few decades later. The Greenland colony would also lose contact in the centuries that followed with the last ship visiting in 1410. Several hundred years later, when a European ship returned there was no sign of the Norse people that had inhabited it. Part of the reason for this failure to maintain a presence was due to the native resistance to their presence and to a drastic change in climate we now call the "Little Ice Age" which caused the already difficult northern sea lanes at the Scandinavian countries latitude to be basically impassable for over a century.

However, Europeans would return when the global climate warmed and their technology had advanced enough to build larger more durable ships capable of sailing the open seas with more reliability. That re-discovery of the Americas would of course be accomplished by none other than the infamous Christopher Columbus; and that is where the story picks up again:

> The first European settlements in the Americas, beginning with the one founded by Columbus in 1492, were in the West Indies .[1] The island Indians, whose estimated population at the time of their "discovery" exceeded a million, were rapidly exterminated on most islands by disease, dispossession, enslavement, warfare and casual murder. Around 1508 the first colony was founded on the American mainland, at the Isthmus of Panama. Conquest of the two large mainland empires, those of the Aztecs and Incas, followed in 1519-1520 and 1532-1533, respectively. In both conquests European-transmitted epidemics (probably smallpox) made major contributions, by killing the emperors themselves, as well as a large fraction of the population. The overwhelming military superiority of even tiny numbers of mounted Spaniards, together with their political skills at exploiting divisions within the native population, did the rest. European conquest of the remaining native states of Central America and northern South America followed during the 16th and 17th centuries.[2]

Master Navigator and Genocidal Governor

Christopher Columbus was born in Genoa, Italy in 1451 and died

1 This area "the West Indies" was so named because of Columbus' original mistaken assumptions that he had arrived in India. This is also the origin of the mislabeling of the Native tribes of North America as Indian, to which the term Amerindian is derived. It is now more commonly known as "the Caribbean" which includes the islands, chains of islands and archipelago from the Gulf of Mexico on the west and stretches out into the Atlantic Ocean on the east, with Florida dangling into the area from the north and its southern border being the continent of South America.

2 Guns, Germs and Steel p.358

on May 20, 1506 in Valladolid, Spain. He was a master navigator and admiral whose four transatlantic voyages (1492–93, 1493–96, 1498–1500, and 1502–04) opened the way for European exploration, exploitation, and colonization of the Americas. He has long been called the "discoverer" of the New World, although Vikings such as Leif Eriksson had visited North America five centuries earlier and monks may have made the journey even earlier without leaving settlements or significant archaeological evidence marking their visit. Columbus made his transatlantic voyages under the sponsorship of Ferdinand II and Isabella I, the Catholic Monarchs of Aragon, Castile, and Leon in Spain. He was at first full of hope and ambition, an ambition partly gratified by his title "Admiral of the Ocean Sea," awarded to him in April 1492, and by the grants enrolled in the Book of Privileges (a record of his titles and claims). However, he died a disappointed man (Encyclopedia Britannica).

The reality of his failed endeavours and the frustration he felt at accidentally discovering North America, rather than reaching the Orient has been glossed over by history. In fact, the man was largely a forgotten historical figure who was recovered and glorified by an American writer in the nineteenth century who was looking for 'American heroes' to celebrate. The re-written history took hold and a holiday 'Columbus Day' was declared in his honour, but the facts of his life do not lie. He invested his fortune, his mind, his time and his life in the pursuit of a lucrative trade route from Europe to India and China, but did not find it. When he did not arrive at his intended destination and found no spices, silks, or precious metals there, he exploited the natives. When they had nothing to offer that had value by current European standards he abused them, enslaved them and killed them. That is the true legacy of Columbus and why the anniversary of his discovery continues to spark protest and indignation across the United States.

The Seven Years' War

This war is often considered the first truly world war, as it was fought between the rival British and French Empires in multiple theaters across the globe. This conflict would end in an overall British victory and mark another leap in Great Britain's ascent to super power status, firmly establishing the British Empire as a premier European state. The English-French competition on land and sea had evolved over the centuries with France normally having the advantage in population, land area and economic power; however, the Seven Years' War would change that balance permanently. Fighting broke out on several continents and on the oceans between them, the British military, especially its navy, demonstrated the strength of its leadership and its personnel in combating the French forces. The fearsome reputation of the British Red Coats as a visible sign of Great Britain's power and authority would also be embedded in the international community of the Imperial Age during the conflict. The Red Coat uniform was first used by the parliamentary New Model Army in the English Civil war, but it was not until the eighteenth century unfolded that it became an enduring symbol of British Imperialism. The aspect of this war that this book is most concerned with is the North American theater this war where it was known as the "French and Indian War." Its resolution came at the Battle of Quebec in 1759, where General Wolfe sacrificed his life in a successful bid to bring the French to a decisive confrontation. For the Native Americans this was a disaster, even for the Iroquois who were allied with the British, as the French had a much more native-friendly colonial policy and a better attitude in general. In addition, the British victory lead to a monopolization of colonial power in North America, which meant that the natives could not use competition between European states to balance expansion.

This British victory meant the European colonists were subjected to a firmer hand from the mother country. The British would soon be imposing new tariffs, taxes and duties to pay for the massive cost of the worldwide conflict, setting the stage for colonial protests, revolts and finally outright rebellion in the form of the American Revolutionary War beginning in 1775. Just twelve years after the Treaty of Paris (1763) had ceded control of New France to Great Britain, the British would be at war again with an even greater challenge then the French soldiers stationed in North America; fighting themselves. Ultimately, British North America would be divided into Upper and Lower Canada in the north and the United States of America in the south, spelling disaster for all North American tribes as the American government released the settlers from the laws prohibiting westward expansion and settlement in Native territory.

The War of Independence

No taxation without representation

So who were the men that insisted on separating from the empire and who drove this effort to establish the first modern democracy? How did this long shot finally come to fruition? It was a long and arduous process before it finally reaped the seeds of rebellion and revolution to emerge as a newly minted independent republic, defeating the British Empire on its own land and on its own terms. There were many reasons for the victory of the colonists and the continental armies, but before the trends and forces are discussed any further the exceptional leadership of several of the most influential figures needs to be mentioned. This star-spangled cast would somehow overcome all the hurdles and obstacles thrown up by the home country and deal with the problems within the colonies themselves at the same time. Only a few of the most prominent of the many capable men will be discussed here, but who better to start the roll call than the eldest of elder statesmen: Benjamin Franklin.

Benjamin Franklin

Benjamin Franklin is one of the most well-known Founding Fathers, not because his face is plastered on the highest denomination of American currency; the one hundred dollar bill, nor is it because wealthy and successful Americans have quiped, "It's all about the Benjamins, baby." It is because of his remarkable intelligence and his success in many disciplines, as well as his major contributions to American independence.

Being almost a generation older than the majority of the other members of the Continental Congress basically made him the Founding Fathers' father, in a manner of speaking. Initially, he was not supportive of a complete break with the mother country, Great Britain, but some seriously negative experiences as a diplomatic representative of the colonies in the English parliament changed his mind. After the revolution began to pick up steam he was posted in Paris where the French promptly fell in love with his native intelligence and charm. He is most famous for inventing the lightning rod, but he was also multi-lingual, a successful businessman, as well as a skillful politician in America and abroad. He was a true polymath and excelled at almost everything he did. In fact, one could argue that without Benjamin Franklin the French would not have entered the war, and if the French had not entered the war the Americans would not have won. Therefore, a sound argument can be made that: no Benjamin Franklin, no American Revolution: The Founding Fathers' father.

General Washington

George Washington, also called 'Father of His Country' was born February 22 in Westmoreland county, Virginia and was, among other things, an American general and the commander in chief of the thirteen colonies' continental armies in the American Revolution from 1775 to 1783 and the first elected President of the United States of America from 1789 to 1797.

Now, when it comes to George Washington it is difficult to separate the man from the myth, but it is important to get the facts straight and to portray him realistically. He was in fact born a British man, in Virginia, which actually makes him a Southerner to boot. This should not be surprising though because on the eve of the American

Revolution Virginia was the most populous and wealthiest colony in America. He was also independently wealthy due to the large tracts of land he owned and the slaves he had working it for him. This allowed him to offer his services to the Continental Congress *pro bono*[3] which, along with his experience as an officer in the British army, convinced them to appoint him commander in chief, a decision they would not regret.

Besides often being considered the greatest American of all-time, being an all-around hero and being revered as a demi-god as much in his own time as he is now, George Washington never told a lie. Nor did he ever curse. Which, unfortunately, is itself a lie! Although he was not always truthful, it is true that he avoided lying as much as was humanly possible and only cursed when he was pushed to the absolute limits of his patience. He was being mythologized before his soul even departed the Earth and his ranking atop the most respected American figures of all time has never wavered, despite the ignominy of his slave ownership and the revelation of his character flaws (he was known to be a very proud man). So, despite the man not quite living up to the myth, there is still a lot to impress in the story of George Washington. After all, he did have the charisma, resilience and vision to lead the continental forces to the completion of a seemingly impossible task: defeating the British army and winning the American Revolutionary War.

3 A Latin term used in legal circles meaning "for free."

Enshrined in this document are the constitutional rights of American citizens and the responsibilities and limitations of the government of the people. It has been amended many times and it fell short of protecting certain people's rights in many ways, In addition to the racial and gender discrimination in the constitution is a clear class discrimination that excluded many loyal British colonists as well. Still, at its heart it still contained principles that elevated the new republic above the conditions of any other 18th century western state. In that sense it was truly revolutionary.

The constitution was a compromise between slaveholding interests of the South and moneyed interests of the north. For the purpose of uniting the 13 states into one great market for commerce, the northern delegates wanted laws regulating interstate commerce, and urged that such laws require only a majority of Congress to pass. The South agreed to this, in return for allowing the trade and slaves to continue for 20 years before being outlawed.

Charles Beard warned us that governments including the government of the United States are not neutral, that they represent the dominant economic interests, and that their constitutions are intended to serve these interests. One of his critics (Robert E. Brown, *Charles Beard and the Constitution*) raises interesting point. Granted that the constitution omitted the phrase "life, liberty and the pursuit of happiness," which appeared in the Declaration of Independence and substituted "life, liberty and property"— well why shouldn't the Constitution protect property? As Brown says about Revolutionary America "practically everybody was interested in the protection of property" because so many Americans owned property. However, this is misleading. True there were many property owners, but some people had much more than others. A few people had great amounts of property; many people had small amounts; others had none. [4]

The After Effects of the American Revolution

The United States of America, created through the efforts of the 13 colonies and its leaders, founded the first modern democracy by conducting a revolutionary war against the British crown. Achieving that full separation and acknowledgment from the mother country in 1783 created a nation that would eventually become the most powerful in the history of the world. The seeds of this revolution had already been sewn in the Reformation and the English Civil War, and was propelled forward with no small influence from the French Revolution. In fact, the French Revolution, as it is studied as the linchpin of modern politics, nationalism, democracy and natural rights[5] in the western European world, occurred in parallel with the American Revolution. These ideas were combined with an incredibly talented cohort produced this result. At no time in American history has there

4 Howard Zinn. A People's History of the United States p. 98

5 This is by no means an exhaustive list.

been more capable, driven, intelligent and charismatic leaders as there were at its inception. A veritable pantheon of great men contributed to the formation of this new nation in North America: and we now remember them as the Founding Fathers. Now only a few of these first great Americans are described in detail in this book, but let us instead focus on a brief overview of how American culture evolved after its revolutionary war was successfully concluded.

In the immediate aftermath of the American War of Independence[6] the colonists who had remained loyal to the British crown and supported remaining in the British Empire found themselves discriminated against. Shunned by the Americans who had sacrificed themselves to break free of the British yoke, many of them elected to immigrate to British North America and settle in what is now Ontario, but was then called Upper Canada. This large movement of loyalist citizens created a balance between the numbers of English-speaking people and French-speaking people in British North America and laid the foundation for the eventual creation of the nation of Canada. So, inadvertently, the American victory gave birth to two nations, not one.

For the Americans independence from the British Empire meant political freedom, but it did not mean economic freedom. In fact, they now found themselves tied even closer to British trade as a foreign state and they were almost entirely dependent on British shipping without much leverage against tariffs or taxation. The irony was real, as the

6 The American War of Independence and the American Revolutionary War are names that are used interchangeably throughout this book.

newly enfranchised American citizens could freely trade with any country, but with the British controlling the seas this was not realistic. In addition, many of the benefits that had come along with being part of the British Empire, such as protection, diplomatic alliances, investment and political support, were no longer provided. For the newfound republic it was a rough go of it initially, to say the least, and the union nearly failed shortly after its inauguration. However, the states began to knit themselves together and the United States began to take shape. It began to build its own merchant marine and aggressively expand westward and southward, despite the difficulties.

Slavery

Before going further, it must be noted though that there was a significant obstacle that threatened the very existence of America from the very beginning. The disparity of wealth and the privilege of one race (and one gender and one class) that discriminated against all others was a near fatal flaw that has threatened the cohesion of America throughout its existence. The most egregious example of America's tendency to discriminate was the slave trade, which continued to be lucrative for the southern states, but was increasingly less appealing to the northern states. This divide through the country's geographical and ideological heart reflected the fundamental differences in social and economic systems between the north and south. Industrialization gradually began to take root in the north whereas plantations still dominated in the agricultural south. Thus, from the beginning, the American identity was characterized by this duality. In time some would call it a two-headed giant, as the specter of its global importance began to grow. However, industrialization using cheap labour began to take root in the north, whereas plantations using slave labour continued to dominate in the agricultural south, the fractured American identity, which was characterized by a duality from the beginning, began its inexorable march toward civil war. Internationally America preferred to remain neutral, which was an idea born from the mind of George Washington himself who disdained to participate in the intricate alliances and wars of the Europeans, having personally experienced them. As a result of that first impulse by its first government the newly created nation was, in essence, isolationist. This was a tricky thing to navigate as the French expected a real alliance and tangible commitments, but over time the young United States was able to withdraw itself and avoid being entangled in the diplomatic web of Europe. This attitude rang true in the famous words of John Quincy Adams, the sixth President of the United States when he warned, "...she [The United States] goes not abroad, in search of monsters to destroy."[7] The prospect of domestic discord hung over the newfound nation as it three critical issues darkened the otherwise bright future of

7 A short excerpt taken from documents relating to American foreign policy. John Quincy Adams, An Historic Address on American foreign policy *Warning Against the Search for "Monsters to Destroy,"* when acting as Foreign Secretary of Stateof the U.S.A. July 4, 1821

America, and it turned out to be last in this short list that would almost rend the country apart and cause it to self-destruct: a solution to the ongoing conflicts with native North American people; the negotiation of international relations; and resolving the fundamental differences between the colonies (now become states).

This is something that people born in the post-World War era need to understand when they look back to the early years of the United States because of the current American reputation for hyper-intervention. In the late 18th century America was an inward looking state, mostly concerned with stabilizing itself and maintaining its own territorial integrity while rapidly expanding over a continent that seemed nearly endless. But by the end of the 19th century there would be an increased interest in participating in the global scramble for colonies and then a massive contribution to both World Wars followed by huge commitments of direct force that would completely change the international geo-political game for America.

Two hundred years ago America was essentially a sleeping giant, much like the sleeping dragon label used to described China in the early 21st century. Everyone could see the potential for America to emerge as a global superpower, but no one could guess how it will play out. As the 19th century unfolded the United States slowly played its hand and gradually awakened from its isolationist stupor. Its momentum carried into the 20th century and it realized its full potential as the greatest superpower the world has ever seen by mid-century. Nonetheless, it is important to remember that just as Abraham Lincoln had his modest start in a log cabin, but was raised to the presidency, so too did the powerful nation-state of America have humble beginnings as a struggling network of colonies clinging to the Atlantic coast, attempting to detach itself from Great Britain. The evolution of American culture, though it began much earlier, made a great leap forward in its revolutionary years, which set the tone for the next two centuries.

America in Shackles

Slavery is a dehumanising, undignified system of forced labor without consent or payment. Some states of slavery are less cruel than others; this is true, but the ownership and control over another human being is fundamental and central to its purpose. The British and American version of slavery practiced in North America is called chattel slavery, which is a particularly demeaning form involving chains and violence to keep the enslaved in line. In a further cruel discriminatory practice, the American version was justified by religion and ideas of racial superiority based on the colour of a person's skin leading to an entire class of people being imported from Africa and subjugated along racial lines.

> [The] transatlantic slave trade, segment of the global slave trade that transported between 10 million and 12 million enslaved Africans across the Atlantic Ocean to the Americas from the 16th to the 19th century [was immense]. It was the second of three stages of the so-called triangular trade in which arms, textiles, and wine were shipped

> from Europe to Africa, slaves from Africa to the Americas, and sugar and coffee from the Americas to Europe.
>
> Probably no more than a few hundred thousand Africans were taken to the Americas before 1600. In the 17th century, however, demand for slave labour rose sharply with the growth of sugar plantations in the Caribbean and tobacco plantations in the Chesapeake region in North America. The largest numbers of slaves were taken to the Americas during the 18th century, when, according to historians' estimates, nearly three-fifths of the total volume of the transatlantic slave trade took place (Encyclopedia Britannica).

The embedded racism begun by slavery continued in official law until Abraham Lincoln's emancipation proclamation freed the slaves and the conclusion of the American Civil War forced the states in the South to accept it too. Unfortunately, this was not the end of the discrimination born out of slavery and the racism and segregation has continued, Even though the Civil Rights movement in the 1960s made more progress, racism remains a serious issue. It is important to understand the background of these social problems and how ingrained discrimination still goes on in the United States today and how it contradicts the essential spirit and basic precepts of equality and human rights expounded in the constitution. When the descendants of slaves, immigrants and all minorities protest, revolt and push for change, it is because they are being restricted and oppressed by a system that still perpetuates inequality. This perspective needs to be understood. as does the term systemic racism as it operates without the conscious knowledge or intent of many American citizens.

British and American Culture:
Evolution and Revolution

Chapter 05

From Sea to Shining Sea

Chapter 05

From Sea to Shining Sea

Great Britain and Her Dominions

The British, though deeply affected by the loss of their American colonies, hardly skipped a beat as they engaged in a final series of conflicts with the French for undisputed Atlantic world domination. This would see them rise to the task militarily, politically and perhaps most importantly, commercially, in confronting one of the greatest leaders of all-time, Napoleon Bonaparte. Some historians have seen the 18th century as the second Hundred Years' War as the French and British Empires fought seven wars, with the British clearing winning five of those seven. The final conclusion would be unambiguous in the Battle of Waterloo, with the French army scattered, Napoleon captured and a general peace reigning over Europe for nearly a century. British North America would consolidate and become Canada, eventually making it the second largest nation on Earth, but the real prize, the crown jewel of the empire as it were, would be India. Thus, the above globe's focus of the United States of America represents an ironic misdirection of focus, as it would not be until the mid 20th Century that North America would briefly claim its sole super power status. In truth, it would be Asia that brought Britain to the height of its power and it would be Asia that began to re-assert its centrality in the twenty-first century.

The British North America Act of 1867

On this momentous occasion a new country was born, but in a remarkably peaceful and diplomatic fashion. Through this act the parliament of the United Kingdom caused three separately operating colonies to merge; Nova Scotia, New Brunswick and Upper/Lower Canada to become a new dominion preparing the way for territories in British North America to join in the future. This act was essentially the beginning of the nation of Canada and its official acceptance on July 1st, 1867 is celebrated as an official national holiday Canada Day. The final stage of this constitutional process was the Canadian Constitution Act of 1982, which is part of the final stages of its evolution away from the main branch of British culture in becoming an almost completely disconnected sovereign state:

> The British North America Act conferred on the new dominion a constitution "similar in principle to that of the United Kingdom." The executive government was vested in Queen Victoria and her successors. These two provisions meant that Canada would have parliamentary and cabinet government. The legislature was to consist of a Senate, its members appointed for life from the regions of Canada, and a House of Commons elected from the provinces on the principle of representation by population. The act provided that criminal law should be federal and civil law provincial. The federal government was to appoint all senior judges, the provinces to administer the laws and maintain the courts. The act also authorized establishment of a Supreme Court of Canada.
>
> The allocation of powers between the federal and provincial governments was done by sections 91 and 92 of the act. By the former, the federal legislature was given power to legislate for "the peace, order and good government of Canada," and "for greater certainty" 29 subjects of exclusive federal jurisdiction were listed.

The act also gave the federal government the right to disallow any provincial act within two years of its passage. The provinces might levy direct taxation only, whereas the dominion might use any mode of taxation. The act thus provided for a union in which the federal government had general and overriding powers, while the provinces had particular and restricted ones.

The course of judicial interpretation in the Judicial Committee of the imperial Privy Council nevertheless transformed the character of the federal constitution under the act by greatly reducing the powers of the federal government and correspondingly increasing those of the provinces. The act provided no process of amendment. Amendments were made by the imperial Parliament in London at the request of the Parliament of Canada (Encyclopedia Britannica).

An old map of the world marked in Latin with the Northwest passage and the coast of British Columbia to Alaska and the Bering Strait yet unexplored.

The Canadian National Anthem

Official English	*Official French*	*Translation from French by the Parliamentary translation bureau*
O Canada! Our home and native land! True patriot love in all thy sons command. With glowing hearts we see thee rise, The True North strong and free! From far and wide, O Canada, we stand on guard for thee. God keep our land glorious and free! O Canada, we stand on guard for thee. O Canada, we stand on guard for thee.	Ô Canada! Terre de nosaïeux, Ton front estceint de fleuronsglorieux! Car ton bras sait porter l'épée, Il sait porter la croix! Ton histoire estuneépopée Des plus brillants exploits. Et ta valeur, de foitrempée, Protégeranos foyers et nos droits. Protégeranos foyers et nos droits.	O Canada! Land of our ancestors Glorious deeds circle your brow For your arm knows how to wield the sword Your arm knows how to carry the cross; Your history is an epic Of brilliant deeds And your valour steeped in faith Will protect our homes and our rights, Will protect our homes and our rights.

The flag pictured here is the one adopted by Canada in 1965. It was and still is somewhat unique among the former commonwealth nations because it only includes two colours and does not reference the Union Jack or Great Britain anywhere in its design. The maple leaf in the center is meant to represent the provinces and territories that comprise the land of Canada, while the red borders on the left and right represent the Pacific and Atlantic oceans respectively.

The Tall Tale and American Folklore

From the formation of British North America, let us now return to the dramatic creation of a new culture and the myth-making endeavours it felt were a necessary part of that process. Even though the United States of America is a relatively new country, if we are to date it from the American Revolutionary War's conclusion in 1783, its mythology stretches back much further than the 18th century. As other nations and cultures have done, the Americans have attempted to root themselves in a mythological past. This myth building project has been just as essential to the formation of American identity as it has been for older cultures and civilizations. The legends, whether exaggerated, partially true or complete fiction, have come down to us through the centuries and informed our understanding of American culture, just as it has informed the understanding of Americans themselves. "Tall Tales" in particular, the quintessential exaggerated story by definition, have come to occupy that special place in America's heart where the humble, stalwart and powerful American hero lives. The movement towards cultural, social and political unification was particularly challenging in the United States and contradictions have arisen which have had to be resolved, put off or ignored altogether. So these myths served to bind the people of diverse heritages in a common American past. As examples of this story-telling, origin spinning, unifying effort, two of the most famous men in American history will be described here: Paul Bunyan and Davy Crockett. The former is the main character in a series of Tall Tales about the expansion of American territory, whereas the latter was a real man whose legend grew and whose exploits were exaggerated.

Paul Bunyan was a giant lumberjack, a mythical hero of the lumber camps in the United States, and a symbol of size, strength, and vitality. The tales and anecdotes that form the Paul Bunyan legend are typical of the tradition of frontier tall tales. Paul and his companions, Babe the Blue Ox and Johnny Inkslinger, are undismayed by rains that last for months, giant mosquitoes, or adverse geography. The tales describe how Paul, who fashions lakes and rivers at will, created Puget Sound, the Grand Canyon, and the Black Hills. They celebrate the lumbermen's prodigious appetites. Paul's camp stove covers an acre, and his hotcake griddle is so large that it is greased by men using sides of bacon for skates (Encyclopedia Britannica).

Although the Alamo has become legendary for its tragic sacrifice in the Texas Revolution of 1836, it was a real event and a pivotal one at that. Many brave men took a stand at the Battle of the Alamo, including Davy Crockett, who gave his life in its defence. The Texian defenders were overrun and most of them slain by the Mexican army, but they inflicted heavy casualties on the attackers. The defeat at the Alamo sparked a rush to join the army in Texas, and ultimately strengthened it. The story was written, drawn, retold and spread across American culture over the years, ensuring it would never be forgotten: "Remember the Alamo" eventually became a hit single originally written and recorded and performed by Donovan. The building in the picture above is a national historical site and a popular tourist attraction in Texas.

The War Between the States

The American Civil War (1861-1865) erupted not long after the election of Abraham Lincoln, the anti-slavery northern President, as several southern states seceded from the union. Complex emotions tend to rise to the surface on all sides when the topic of the Civil War is broached and the perspectives and emotions invoked can be very polarizing. In 2017, on the History channel website,[1] experts from across the United States of America were asked to sum up the conflict in one word. There were a myriad of suggestions including: 'freedom,' 'bloody,' 'heroic,' 'fortunate,' 'unintended,' 'unfinished' or 'tragic.' Since there appears to be little consensus on how we should interpret and remember the American Civil War, even among experts including historians, professors and curators, how can a textbook be expected to portray this event properly? It is a daunting task, but in this short space, as with so much of the content in this book, an attempt will be made at giving multiple perspectives and doing some small justice to this epoch defining period.

The differences in the culture of the American urban industrial north and the American rural agricultural south had been brewing and stewing underneath, barely kept from being directly expressed outside of political circles and in confrontations in broad daylight. However, it would soon be openly declared, defended and asserted by both sides.

1 www.history.com

The Union and the Confederacy would fight in politics and on the battlefield, until one was forced to submit to the other's superiority of arms; and therefore, ideology.

There is one thing that all the experts agree on when it comes to the American Civil War; it was momentous and significant. The "War Between the States" threatened to tear the United States apart as much as it promised to reward a final victor with a unified nation. How would the country treat the defeated and how would it heal after so much had been thrown into its own destruction? This is as good a place as any to start, as the citizens of the United States were drawn into a war that had initially seemed a typical political spat, but rapidly escalated into the bloodiest, deadliest, costliest war in American history in terms of human casualties by raw numbers. Approximately 620,000 men were killed in military conflicts during the war which represented 2% of the population at the time. That figure also does not include the many thousands of civilians that died of various causes including disease, displacement, starvation and being caught in the line of fire.

18th century cannons side by side still guarding a fort, but now frozen and ringed by chains as a museum's monument to the great conflicts of the past. These cannons are not unlike the ones wheeled onto the battlefield in the American Civil War and by Napoleon in Europe sixty years beforehand.

"Its Glory is All Moonshine."

William Tecumseh Sherman was said to utter this phrase after he took a Union army on a looping march into the South in an effort to get at the infrastructure of the Confederacy. In his own words he claimed he would make "Georgia howl." Unbeknownst to the Union generals and the government of the North, the Confederate army was just as war weary as their own. The rioting and resistance to conscription in the north, was mirrored by the thousands of small land farmers who formed the bulk of the Confederate army. The wealthy upper class continued to dig in their heels, but the core of the army in the South was undersupplied, underfed, and now outnumbered and outgunned. When General Sherman began his march through Georgia to Atlanta, employing a scorched earth policy, it was none too soon for either side as the rank and file soldiers were nearing the breaking point:

> When recruiting for the army began in July 1863, a mob in New York wrecked the main recruiting station. Then, for three days, crowds of white workers marched through the city, destroying buildings, factories, streetcar lines, homes. The draft riots were complex—anti-black, anti-rich, anti-Republican. From an assault on draft headquarters, the rioters went on to attacks on wealthy homes, then to the murder of blacks. They marched through the streets, forcing factories to close, recruiting more members of the mob. They set the city's colored orphan asylum on fire. They shot, burned, and hanged blacks they found in the streets. Many people were thrown into the rivers to drown.
>
> On the fourth day, Union troops returning from the Battle of Gettysburg came into the city and stopped the rioting. Perhaps four hundred people were killed. No exact figures have ever been given, but the number of lives lost was greater than any other incident of domestic violence in American history.[2]

This discontent was even more severe in the southern states as the tide of the war began to turn and the northern states began to bring their industrial power and resources to bear. As the war dragged on the most significant disadvantage for the Confederacy became the disparity in troop numbers and low morale. The leaders in the South were

2 Howard Zinn. A People's History of the United States. p.237

reluctant to let African-American slaves fight; as that would require arming them and they feared a revolt, with good reason. However, this meant that they could not match the Union army's numbers and they could not feed, clothe or equip their soldiers as well either. Thus, it was that in many cases, "Behind the rebel battle yells and the legendary spirit of the Confederate army, there was much reluctance to fight."[3] The Civil War was essentially over on April 9, 1865 when Robert E. Lee, general of the Confederate forces, surrendered the army of Northern Virginia to Ulysses S. Grant. Although sporadic fighting would continue and other units would surrender later that year, the end was now a foregone conclusion.

The Final Frontier

With the British expelled and the Civil War concluded, leaving the South in shambles, there was a renewed push westward, which spelled doom for the many aboriginal people already occupying the territory to the west, whether they belonged there, had fled or been forcibly re-located from other land. The American-Indian Wars were the last ditch efforts by the native people to defend their land from the encroachment of Americans, Europeans, colonists and settlers of all kinds. However, despite some cooperation between myriad tribes and heroic efforts by many, it was too late resist American expansion.

3 Howard Zinn. A People's History of the United States. p.237

The California Gold Rush

Part of the impetus for the drive westward was that shiny yellowish metal that has attracted humans for untold generations: gold. The discovery of gold brought prospectors, businessmen, adventurers, investors and people from all walks of life to the west coast where they could try their luck and test their mettle panning for gold in the mountainous reaches of California. Initially the proportion of settlers was fairly balanced, with a mixture of Spanish, natives and newly arriving English along with other Americans, but with the wild rumors of gold nuggets being found in riverbeds migration exploded with men soon outnumbering women in some areas by as many as 10:1. Although there were women who sought their fortune and braved the climate, rocky terrain, wild animals and thieves, most made their living in the entertainment or service business in mining towns, catering to the needs of men. The type of entertainment would vary from town to town, but would normally include singing, dancing, serving food and drink, prostitution, escorting or cleaning. It would take decades before the gender balance in the State would reach equilibrium, but the proportion of women would steadily rise from last days of the Gold Rush to the present.

Side Effects of Rapid Westward Expansion

For many Americans and newly arrived immigrants the American Wild West represented the American dream. In the untamed and unending expanse of the continent there were also unending possibilities. The unattached could seek their fortune through adventure, exploration, prospecting, business, investment or even thievery; after all, untamed also meant lawless. Freed slaves, Irish and other European immigrants, criminals, the destitute, the disavowed; anyone had a chance to start a new life, to start all over while at the same time participating in a national building project. This era would later be romanticized and glorified by American cinema as a period that exemplified the American spirit and the values of toughness, confidence, independence and destiny. The Hollywood portrayals would capture the American imagination and that of the world so completely that the Western genre would dominate the silver screen for decades and re-write historical memory.

But this was not how it really was. Making the journey westward was fraught with danger and there was no guarantee of success once you arrived, wherever it was you were going, or ended up. The government was extending its authority, but settlement by individuals and families continued far in advance of American borders, despite treaties and legal agreements and promises to respect territorial limits. The main problem with this unfettered colonial spirit, drawing its energy from the pre-independence thirteen colony era was that the land was already occupied. True it was sparsely populated compared to European standards, but all the interior of the continent, stretching right to the waves of the Pacific Ocean lapping at the shores of the West Coast, had already been settled thousands of years before; by tribes of native Americans as varied as the new influx of people from the European continent. And just like the Europeans, these people were not unified, and being less populous and without the technology or resources to makes tools and weapons, they fell easy prey to American settlers operating outside the law, where laws were not enforced, or in areas without established laws protecting native American people. The larger tribes or confederations of tribes were confronted directly in the American-Indian Wars by the American government through military force, but what is less well known, but just as disturbing was the treatment of smaller, independent, less-connected or isolated native groups. In his book Guns, Germs and Steel Jared Diamond cites some examples the destructive encroachment on communities, displacement and murderous pursuit of Native Americans that occurred during the mid-nineteenth century in California:

> Smaller native societies were destroyed more casually, by small-scale raids and murders carried out by private citizens. For instance, California's native hunter-gatherers initially numbered about 200,000 in aggregate, but they were splintered among a hundred tribelets, none of which required a war to be defeated. Most of these tribelets were killed off or dispossessed during or soon after the California gold rush of 1848-52, when large numbers of immigrants flooded into the state. As one example, the Yahitribelet of northern California, numbering about 2,000 and lacking firearms, was destroyed in four raids by armed white settlers: a dawn raid on a Yahi village carried out by 17 settlers on August 6, 1865; a massacre of Yahis surprised in a ravine in 1866; a massacre of 33 Yahis tracked to a cave around 1867; and a final massacre of about 30 Yahis trapped in another cave by 4 cowboys around 1868. Many Amazonian Indian groups were similarly eliminated by private settlers during the rubber boom of the late 19th and early 20th centuries. The final stages of the conquest are being played out in the present decade [the 1990s], as the Yanomamo and other Amazonian Indian societies that remain independent are succumbing to disease, being murdered by miners, or being brought under control by missionaries or government agencies.[4]

4 Jared Diamond. Guns, Germs and Steel p. 358-359

One of the most tragic things about the depopulation of the North American native tribes is that they were completely unprepared for the vicious aggressiveness of American expansion. The kill or be killed attitude and the intense competition among Europeans scrambling for money, land and resources was simply alien to most native cultures. The lack of cultural understanding and the inability to organize in the face of the American threat was yet another factor affecting the aboriginal struggle to survive and keep their land:

> The end result has been the elimination of populous Native American societies from most temperate areas suitable for European food production and physiology. In North America those that survived as sizable intact communities now live mostly on reservations or other lands considered undesirable for European food production and mining, such as Arctic and arid areas of the U.S. West. NativeAmericans in many tropical areas have been replaced by immigrants from the Old World tropics (especially black Africans, along with Asian Indians and Javanese in Suriname).[5]

5 Jared Diamond. Guns, Germs and Steel p. 359

A conventional image of the cowboy riding across the plains appearing to be tough, pure, lawful, dignified and honourable. Although probably only the first adjective is accurate; they were indeed tough. They rode in the saddle all day in all manner of weather and slept on the ground. They were also mostly uneducated, dirty, rude and unruly, contrary to the American mythology popularized by the Hollywood Western film genre.

The Original Americans

The original Native American population has been reduced by a debated large percentage: estimates for North America range up to 95 percent. But the total human population of the Americas is now [in 1997] approximately ten times what it was in 1492, because of arrivals of Old World peoples (Europeans, Africans, and Asians). The population of the Americas now consists of a mixture of peoples originating from all continents except Australia. That demographic shift of the last 500 years—the most massive shift on any continent

> except Australia—has its ultimate roots in developments between about 11,000 B.C. and A.D. 1.[6]

This is why it is essential to root a discussion of American culture in its forerunner British culture, and in its predecessor the English, and its ancestors the Norman, Scottish, Irish, Welsh, Dane, Anglo-saxon, Romano-British, Briton, Pictish and even those people that belonged to the original culture of the British Isles that are exemplified in the uncovered ruins in Orkney. Whether one subscribes to Jared Diamond's now famous theory based on the evolutionary advantages of certain geo-political cultural positions leading to germs, guns and steel being the fundamental difference between the eventual balance of power across the continents, or not, this continuum provides us with lessons of universal cultural development that should not be ignored. Theorizing the cause and effect relationships in the history of culture is one thing, and studying what happens when two vastly different cultures at different stages of development come into contact, is another. Studying the outcome of those encounters and the behaviour exhibited by the people in both foreign cultures, in this case the British and American cultures meeting the culture of the North American tribes is, arguably a much more necessary and concrete thing to examine.

The tragic fate for many of the Native North American tribes was

6 Jared Diamond. Gun, Germs and Steel p. 358

to be decimated by disease and the collapse of their societies was a consequence of the sickness and death that spread through their communities:

> As for the most advanced native societies of North America, those of the U.S. Southeast and the Mississippi River system, their destruction was accomplished largely by germs alone, introduced by early European explorers and advancing ahead of them. As Europeans spread throughout the Americas, many other native societies, such as the Mandans of the Great Palins and the Sadlermiut Eskimos of the Arctic, were also wiped out by disease, without need for military action. Populous native societies not thereby eliminated were destroyed the same way the Aztecs and Incas had been—by full-scale wars increasingly waged by professional European soldiers and their native allies. Those soldiers were backed by the political organizations initial of the European mother countries, then of the independent neo-European states that succeeded the colonial governments.[7]

Much has been made of these original encounters and the innocence of the Native Americans in contrast with the desperate lust of the European settlers (the English among them). The result of this contact is that these tribes would not remain neighbours, friends or enemies of the United States, but be converted, absorbed or corralled onto reserves as a permanent part of what we now know as American culture, whether they were willing or not. While abuse, war, crime and even

7 Jared Diamond. Gun, Germs and Steel p. 358

genocide have been common throughout human history it should not, and cannot be excused away because of their frequency. With all due respect to the hundreds of cultures, languages and tribes that are not mentioned here, several groups of Native people will be described below to give a small representative sampling to the reader. There is a strong historical bias in the selection of these North American First Nations groups, as they have been chosen based on their fame, their profound effect on American culture (both real and imagined), their diverse geographical location and on their first contact with European explorers, soldiers, settlers, colonists and pioneers.

A sketch of a Native American Chieftain wearing a feathered headdress, perhaps for ceremonial purposes. Many native tribes had colourful, elaborate costumes for various cultural events and performed traditional dances for spiritual as well as practical reasons.

The Arawaks

The Lucayan-Arawak people were the first to be exposed to the terrible insensitivity of the white man. They inhabited the Bahamas leading a largely peaceful existence, as they were isolated from conflict with other tribes by the sea, so they were completely unprepared for the voracious appetite for gold and the complete disregard for life that Columbus and his crews exhibited. Not long after the first Spanish ships arrived the entire race of people had been enslaved, murdered or killed by disease making them the first victims of European genocide as well, a terrible pattern that would continue with British and American expansion on the North American mainland. Howard Zinn describes how this tragic scene with the innocent first encounter between the European explorers and the natives looked: "Arawak men and women, naked, tiny, and full of wonder, emerge from the villages onto the island beaches and swim out to get a closer look at the strange big boat. When Columbus and his sailors came ashore, during swords, speaking oddly, the Arawaks ran to greet them, brought them food, water, gifts."[8]

8 Howard Zinn. A People's History of the United States.p. 1.

The sketch above is of a typical Native American warrior. He is clad in buckskin and his long hair is tied back. A medallion hangs from his neck and a tomahawk dangles from his hand at his side.

The Iroquois

The Iroquois tribes were famous for being aggressive. They were clever and skilled at hunting and at making war. They often skirmished with the tribes on their borders and with each other, so it should come as no surprise that when the Europeans arrived and they made contact, it led to ever escalating conflict. They allied themselves with the British and Americans in fighting the French and their native counterparts north of the Great Lakes, the Algonquin. Since they were the more war-like, the more numerous people and had stronger allies the Iroquois briefly came to dominate the North East after the defeat of the Algonquin along with their French allies in Nouvelle France before American and Canadian expansion took their territory away piecemeal. Some of the most famous tribes in their confederacy were the Cherokee, Huron, Mohawk, and Seneca.

They had a sophisticated culture which included a complex political system organized by location, age and gender. They often held councils in villages and in larger groups of villages, tribes and "nations." They lived in permanent wooden structures called longhouses that were arranged neatly in clearings. Their lives revolved around family and they had a rich spiritual life that included myths of their origins, superstitions and festivals marking significant points in the year. Their fierce reputation was well-deserved and a man's reputation in their culture was largely dependent on his military prowess. They were adaptable and tenacious fighters who quickly mastered the use of European firearms once they gained access to them through trade. Their pre-colonial population may have been as high as one million people, but the current number of Iroquois descendants is less than ten percent of that number.

This picture depicts various objects crafted by Native Americans. Many more tools and weapons were made by First Nations people in hundreds of tribes and villages. Some of the most famous of them are included here: the tomahawk in the center, the webbed dreamcatchers scattered across the picture, a carved bow, arrows and a peace pope just above the tomahawk.

The Algonquin

Part of the area the Algonquin tribe once occupied is now a provincial park in Ontario, Canada of the same name. It is about 10,000 square km in size. This is but a fraction of the territory that once belonged to them as they roamed the dense forests and rolling hills stretching from Lake Huron to the Ottawa River valley. The traditions of the Algonquin people were quite similar to the other tribes in their region and one can get a sense of their culture and organisation by visiting reconstructed historically accurate villages in modern day northern Ontario. They lived in longhouses constructed of wood and grew corn, caught fish and hunted in bands of warriors across their forested lands. Perhaps the most significant of their domestic cultural practices was their knowledge of the plants and animals that led to their discovery that maple trees could be tapped in the spring for sap. From that sugary tree water they could produce syrup. This original method of making maple syrup was taught to the French and was passed down from them to present day Canadians making the Algonquin the ancestral founders of one of Canada's most identifiable agricultural products.

With respect to the contents of this book, this tribe in particular is relevant as they were the natural enemies of the tribes in the Iroquois Confederacy. They were generally a more peaceful people than the aggressive Iroquois and their geographical location made them the natural allies of the French, who tended to be more forthright in their dealings with natives than other European colonists. The Iroquois allied themselves with the British as the European colonies grew and together they defeated the French-Algonquin alliance in the French and Indian War. Sadly for both the winning (Iroquois) and losing (Algonquin) Native American tribes, their people would fall into decline after the British gained supremacy in North America, a period to be followed by American dominance. As with nearly all Native tribes,[9] they

9 A notable exception is the Inuit people who were able to retain most of their lands largely due to the harsh climate and their remote location.

were gradually dispossessed of their ancestral lands and their culture was overtaken by American and British colonists.The number of Algonquin descendants has been estimated at approximately 5,000 going into the early 21st century, which represents a small fraction of a people that likely easily numbered in the tens of thousands a scant four centuries ago.

The Sioux

The Sioux were a strong and numerous people of plainsmen. They were expert horsemen and excellent marksmen even though the horse was not an animal native to North America and was introduced by the Spanish. They occupied the interior of the North American continent that we now call "the Prairies" and fought some of the biggest battles against European settlement to preserve their territory against American encroachment. Unfortunately, even though their attempts at unifying the diverse tribes occupying the grasslands were successful to a degree, it was too little too late. They would fight a losing battle against the American military and would resist ever more restrictive treaties that were continuously broken during their fighting retreat westward. Eventually they were constrained to reservations out of necessity and had to put themselves at the American government's mercy. Enough of their people remain to tell of the great history of their once powerful and influential cultures. Some of their stoic dignity has been captured in pictures like the one above with the full headdress displayed on the Sioux warriors and the native archer on horseback below.

The Apache

The Apache were one of the last tribes to present organized resistance against the Americans. They were still fighting and going off their reservation in the late 19th century! They were legendary trackers and hunters, masters of camouflage. Of all the Native American tribes they were perhaps, the greatest at conducting the surprise attack, the ambush. At the end of their resistance against American expansion they had no choice but to use guerilla style attacks to strike terror in the settlers near their territory. The American government attempted to deal with them, but raiding was an essential part of their culture and it was inevitable that they would steal, if not be violent toward anyone who settled nearby. Adding to the uniqueness of this Native American tribe was their elaborate rites of passage and their taboo against eating fish. The exoticness of their culture has added to their fame as it only adds to the romanticization of their history.

Geronimo was an Apache chief, and as one of the last Native American Chiefs to fight against the American military, became a celebrity and a legend in his own right when he was finally captured and then brought to meet the President. American people still yell "Geronimo!" when they attempt a dangerous feat such as leaping out of an airplane; such was the influence of the tribe's culture and the reputation of this man. Thus, it is no coincidence the American military has an attack helicopter named the Apache, which has become nearly as famous as the native people themselves.

The Trail of Tears

Eventually all of the tribes had to retreat in the face of the advance of the North American-European civilization. "The trail of tears" is the metaphorical and literal name given to this retreat as the tribes were forced to give up their territory and their way of life. It is the collective responsibility of all humanity to remember these people and their dignity, to include them in their rightful place in American history and culture, as well as to be, at the very least, receptive to and supportive of the recovery of their distinct culture for future generations. There are many other tribes that deserve specific mention in this section of the chapter dedicated to the dignity, influence and decline of the Amerindian culture, but as is the case with many of the people discussed in this book, further study beyond this short summary will do them more justice as they have had an impact that goes far beyond what is described here. The memory of their North American civilisation, their respect for nature and their fierce pride should not be allowed to fade away and should continue on in their descendants.

Collective Guilt

The ongoing struggle to atone for their cultural loss and the abuse of native North Americans that persists into the 21st century continues to be a mark of shame on American culture (and Canadian and Mexican for that matter) just as the segregation and mistreatment of any minority is. At the end of this chapter a map is included that demonstrates how widespread and diverse the Native American tribes were before the European colonists and then American, Canadian and Mexican settlers encroached on their territories. The number of names on the map entitled "Tribes of the Indian Nation" is truly astounding and the loss of the majority of them to history is a painfully tragic part of the narrative of the American nation.

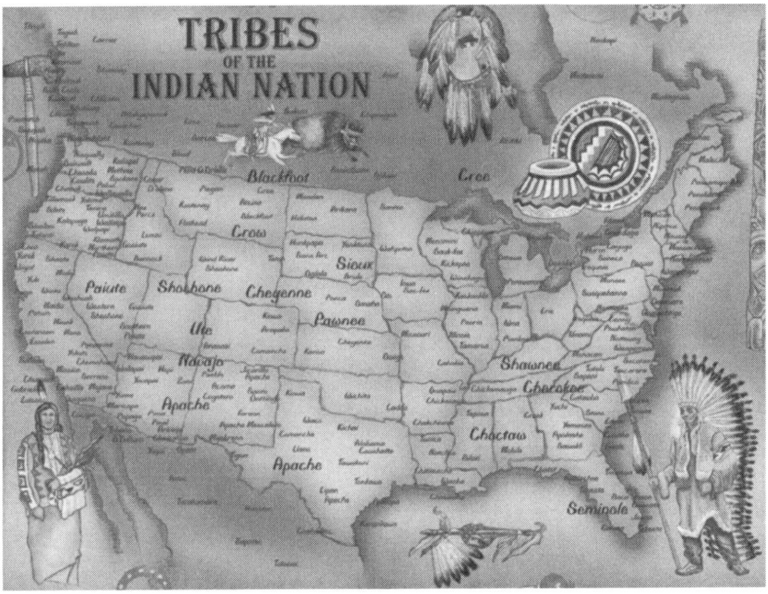

Above is a map of the numerous tribes that are known to have occupied North American territory before being steadily and forcibly moved, corralled or eradicated by colonists and settlers. The larger, more powerful tribes and confederations of tribes that we have more information about are written in larger bold lettering.

British and American Culture:
Evolution and Revolution

Chapter 06

A Tale of Two Empires

Chapter 06

A Tale of Two Empires

Imperial Rule

Imperialism is the idea of a country, kingdom or people extending its power and dominating other territories through colonialism, exploitation of resources and military power. The root of the word is the Latin word Imperium, which means "supreme power." Great Britain became one of the most recent examples of this system in the mid nineteenth century when it began to consolidate its overseas territories with a central administration based out of London. The British were fond of comparing themselves to the original Western imperial power, ancient Rome, so cultural references and similarities abound in their expression and justification of their rule. The domination that the

British exerted over other people across the globe can be seen through multiple lenses, including but not limited to; colonialism, Racism, Orientalism and Social Darwinism.

Benefits and demerits of empire

With an obvious bias towards the benefits of empire the British, with all their efforts to tie themselves to the Empire of the ancient Romans, could paint a convincing picture of how, through their control and leadership, the world could be improved. Among the reasons they listed were the following points: the British Empire:

- Created a period of relative global peace with no major outbreaks of war amongst the world's most powerful states.
- Provided protection from attack and security provided by the Royal Navy and British garrisons
- Opened sea lanes and protected them from pirates and increased trade and business opportunities
- Shared technology, advances in science, education and philosophy between far-flung territories
- Provided access to art, literature and the most sophisticated civilization in the world

However, if you were an original resident of one of the territories dominated by the British Empire, you may have felt differently about the pros and cons of imperial rule. What if, from your perspective, the stability and organization was not a positive thing? What if you already had your own systems in place, and they were displaced by the British one? For many people empire was not advantageous at all, but a clear disadvantage that robbed them of their sovereignty and their dignity. The list of demerits includes, but is not limited to:

- The appropriation of local resources and taxes on goods
- A foreign government controlling your state by the presence of military garrisons and the threat of force
- Having no self-determination as a sovereign state or territory
- A lack of political representation in the British government
- The sacrifice of native languages and education from the dominated area in favor of British culture and learning
- A lack of recognition of the value and importance of culture, art, music and designs that were not British
- The creation of laws enforced by the foreign imperial power

Ireland

Ireland was one of the most notorious victims of British imperial policy and these two tombstones that mark the graves of an Irish couple in a local cemetery are poignant reminders of their struggle for self-determination, for cultural preservation and for independence. One of the many long term consequences, and perhaps the most bitterly contested one, was the lack of home rule in the Irish kingdom. When national catastrophes arose such as the notorious Potato famine of the mid 1800s, there was little the Irish could do to affect their own destiny. Whether the English authorities running the British government acted too slowly, out of ignorance, or out of spite is beside the point. The Irish starved in the hundreds of thousands and were powerless to do anything, but abandon their homeland, or pray for deliverance. This also is the legacy of British imperial culture.

Dress Rehearsal for Empire

Although the Irish also did their share of raiding, especially in the vacuum created by the withdrawal of the Romans from Britannia, there's has largely been a history of *being invaded.* With the Atlantic Ocean at their backs the Irish had to contend with the sea-faring peoples of the east; first the Vikings, then Anglo-saxons, Normans, English and finally the British. The invasion of the Anglo-Normans several generations after William the Conqueror resulted in an English and later British presence that still affects Ireland to this day. The Emerald Isle was conquered many times, but it stubbornly maintained its language, traditions, political ties to the continent, religion and alliances with European states, despite repeated invasions. Irish culture through trade, travel, religious practices and conflict had a strong impact on the development of British culture as the English were always concerned with the Irish question at some level, as they still are. One can pick many dates to mark the end of the Old Gaelic order, but most commonly the "Flight of the Earls" in 1607. The English Government of Ireland took control of Ulster and because of the continued fragmentary nature of the Irish kingdoms a succession of English monarchs and generals, including the infamous Cromwell asserted their authority, often by brutally crushing rebellions and imposing strict laws against the Irish, especially the Catholics. This began a long period of occupation and injustices that provided a test case, if not a model for future British colonial endeavours across the world. For the imperialists it was dominating and neutralizing a foreign threat, for the Irish an unwelcome and ill-intentioned violation of their land, property, religion, rights, freedom; their entire culture was under assault. Many other peoples across the globe would feel similarly toward British colonial projects.

The Rising British Super Power

The Rise of the Machine

This book is entitled "Evolution and Revolution," the reasons for which were explained in the introduction, and we would be remiss if we did not discuss in some detail the largest and most prolonged revolution of them all: the industrial revolution. The first question that must be addressed is whether it was a burst of new innovation that altered British society quickly and then took root in other countries later, or if it was a gradual, slow, step by step process of change; in other words, not a true revolution at all. This debate continues to this day, but according to any strict definition the industrialization of the United Kingdom would appear to be an evolutionary step rather than a revolutionary one. This, industrial legacy, is of all the things that the British have left behind through their dramatic expansion, growth and development into an empire in the modern period, the most widespread and profound, as it is still ongoing over two and a half centuries later.

It was the transition from reliance on man power and domesticated animals to machine power that gave the first industrial nation in the world the advantage it needed on the sea, on land, in tradeand in war to become a first rate global power. An exponential increase in production would occur in the United Kingdom giving it the capacity to outproduce any other country in the world by the mid-19th century. By 1850 it had the largest GDP in the world, even overtaking the Russian Empire with its vast resources and the Chinese Empire with their enormous labor pool.

The key factors that underpinned the Industrial Revolution at its inception were ironmaking technology for building machines, steam power as a source of energy to drive them and the demand for textiles in domestic and foreign markets. Historically, textiles had been produced on the looms in the Netherlands and northern France, while a huge source of the raw material, primarily wool, was mostly from the United Kingdom. However, with the introduction of cotton as a preferred material for all manner of textiles and the creation of a domestic textile industry in England, the conditions were prepared that would change the way that the British worked, and lived, forever:

After the Restoration[1] in 1660, there began in England economic changes that would, for better or worse, transform the life of humanity more than at any time since the prehistoric development of settled agriculture. Over the previous three centuries, total global per capita wealth had increased by less than 50 percent; over the next two centuries, it increased by more than 700 percent. After nearly three centuries of trial and error, much of the world is still trying to follow in England's footsteps. Why did it happen? What were its consequences, good and bad?

The Industrial Revolution—a term from the 1820s—has left a mixed reputation in our national memory. If it made England what Disraeli called "the workshop of the world," it did so by means of William Blake's "dark, satanic mills," squalid towns, and a degraded and exploited workforce. That at least was the belief of many at the time and since. As England changed, it cherished a cult of unspoiled nature, and it has retained ever since a bittersweet nostalgia for Thomson's "Sylvan life,"[2] a pre-industrial arcadia. We see it in art, literature, music and politics; in England's lack of love for its big towns; in the protective passion for "picture postcard" villages; in the ersatz rusticity of the suburbs; and in the widespread taste for rural holiday homes and mass devotion to the National Trust. Not least, we see it in the way English history is written. Yet while deploring their own ancestors' fate the English applaud the industrializing efforts of developing countries which have created cities far bigger, filthier, more unequal and more crowded than the worst Industrial England ever managed.[3]

1 This refers to the restoration of the Stuart monarchy in England, Scotland and Ireland when Charles II was made king.

2 A reference to James Thomson's "The Castle of Indolence" (1748).

3 Robert Toombs. The English and Their History. p.369-370

So, the Industrial Revolution propelled countries into the Modern Age, but at what cost? The costs and benefits of the process, not just in Great Britain and the United States, but all around the world, have long been debated. Often we are focused on the economic and technological changes that it brought about, but consider the two iconic pictures below and reflect on the consequences on society and the environment.

One of the most important elements that contributed to the amazing increase in industrial capacity in the United Kingdom was iron-working. This technology was also developed early on by the Swedish, but the British truly harnessed its strength by mass producing machines of this new stronger material. Eventually this would lead to steel production, which is pictured above. This new technology would require tools and machines made from iron ore to produce in any sizeable quantity.

Evolving Industries

> Though long term the global consequences, good and bad, of the Industrial Revolution are obvious, the immediate effects on England and its people are less so. This has long been a vexed question. From the beginning there were enemies of the new economy, who attacked it on moral, social, aesthetic and eventually ideological grounds. It was corrupting, encouraging luxury and vice; it was disruptive and ugly. Others had praised "commercial society," most famously the Scottish philosophers David Hume and Adam Smith, who asserted that the new economy remedied poverty and unemployment and its "obvious and simple system of natural liberty" provided the basis for a peaceful, civilized, cooperative and stable society. Individual self-betterment would serve the general good as if by "an invisible hand": "It is not from the benevolence of the butcher, or the baker, that we expect our dinner, but form their regard to their own self-interest" So economic freedom was not only right, it was also productive. Oppression and slavery were not only wrong, but also inefficient. Pessimistic and optimistic interpretations have continued ever since, and have shaped English social and political ideas.[4]

To give a balanced answer to this question is very difficult no matter how much analysis is done as the Industrial Revolution was a "soft revolution" that occurred gradually over time, which in this book has been labeled "evolution." Some of the changes and processes still ongoing today and economists, historians and sociologists the world over are now fond of dividing it into stages.[5] It is also a matter

4 Robert Tombs. p. 379

5 By the reckoning of Klaus Schwab that has been popularized in the twenty first century, we are now entering the fourth industrial revolution.

of prioritizing economic development over social and environmental preservation if one is to examine rapid industrial development from a more positive perspective viewpoint, so there will likely never be a proper consensus on the subject. However; if there is any criticism that sticks on this subject it is the emphasis placed on its adverse effects on the majority of people in terms of social welfare, health and quality of life:

> The fundamental question is whether the Industrial Revolution improved or damaged the lives of the English people as a whole. "Optimists" could point to the undeniable increase in living standards that took place—eventually. They inferred that technology and increased economic activity must have increased wealth. "Pessimists" argue that industrialization for many decades brought workers little but cost them much—loss of independence and self-respect, devaluation of skills, deteriorating health, high mortality, bad food, crushing labour (for men, women and children), and destruction of cherished customary rights and community traditions. In short, the Industrial Revolution created an impoverished, downtrodden and embittered proletariat, ground down by the power of money and the oppression of the ruling classes, and forced by long and bitter struggle to assert their meagre rights to a share in national wealth.[6]

The Second Agricultural Revolution

A major influence on the explosive growth that the British saw

6 Howard Zinn. A People's History of the United States. p. 379

in 18th century dated back to the 17th in which farming techniques improved producing food surpluses. This event preceded the British Industrial Revolution and continued alongside it allowing the population to avoid the Malthusian trap.[7] There was a feedback relationship between the two gradual non-violent revolutions as new innovations spurred growth. As land became managed better through crop rotation, yields increased. The Dutch acquired an iron plough which was more effective at turning over soil, and that tool spread across Europe improving agriculture production further. Transportation systems allowed produce to be shipped regionally and then nationally and these markets supported domestic farmers. Land that had previously been seen as unfarmable was drained, reclaimed or otherwise improved. Selective breeding produced animals that were better fit for meat, milk, wool or other animal products. The desired traits then became widespread as animals were bred to be healthier, hardier and larger. Finally, fields were enclosed making them more efficient and thus requiring less labor. However, just as in the case of the Industrial Revolution, there were trade-offs. Enclosure in particular was unpopular as many herdsmen and peasants lost their jobs, which in some cases their families had been doing for generations. The transformation of agricultural practices increased the migration of people to cities and the rapid urbanization of England, which had

7 A theory proposed by Reverend Robert Thomas Malthus that predicts that population increase will outpace food production resulting in mass starvation.

many negative side effects including overcrowding, disease, traffic congestion, unsanitary conditions and social conflicts. Along with the Industrial Revolution this caused a slow, but dramatic shift in British culture from a rural agrarian lifestyle to an industrialized urban culture.

Capitalism & Adam Smith

In many societies throughout the world, particularly in the United Kingdom and the United States, capitalism is ubiquitous. It is often considered not only the best economic system, but the only real option. However, this was not always so. The British Isles adopted a variety of economic systems throughout its history according to its needs, its trade relations and its political system. Adam Smith, a Scottish born philosopher and economist, claimed that, "Great nations are never impoverished by private, though they sometimes are by public prodigality and misconduct. The whole, or almost the whole public revenue, is in most countries employed maintaining unproductive hands."[8] As a precursor to the entire field of modern economics that moved away from mercantilism and protectionism that favored taxes, tariffs and government interference or regulation. Adam Smith was a proponent of the free market and the so-called invisible hand that provided market growth and stability. The financial revolution followed these kinds of theories enabled the British to function on

8 Smith, Adam. 282–283

credit, borrow, loan and insure. It provided the stability and economic expansion to outspend France, outfight Napoleon and construct a global empire.

This factory could be considered the great grandchild of its smaller, dirtier ancestors that were born in northern Europe. Eventually the mass production started in the British Industrial Revolution took hold across Europe and then in North America. Now the process continues in Asia, South America and Africa as nations continue to industrialize using ever increasing amounts of energy and doing ever more damage to the environment.

Romanticism

Romanticism was an intellectual and artistic movement that emphasized the individual, inspiration and nature. It reacted to the power, perspective and speed of the industrial movement, that seemed to have a dehumanising, if not a corrupting effect. It opposed rationalism, realism and then modernism as it sought truth in nature and in the mind. Two of its chief English proponents were William Wordsworth and Samuel Coleridge, whose highly praised Lyrical Ballads collection of poetry and their emphasis on the preservation of the environment has left a legacy of beautiful writing and the National Trust known as the the Lake District in the northern western England.

Mastering the World's Oceans

Coincidental with the British Industrial Revolution was its rise to prominence on the sea. Initially this was an institutional advantage with a better trained, more effective and more experienced navy than other nations, but it soon acquired a production capacity and technological advantage over its rivals as well. Arthur Herman introduces the power and influence of the British imperial navy like this:

> The job of the historian isn't just to recount or explain the past but to show how things have come to be what they are. This book will show how a single institution, the British Navy, built the modern global system, which is our system, for better or worse. It did this first by challenging and toppling the global system forged by Spain and Portugal in the age of Columbus, then it reshaped the world in the 18th and 19th centuries to fit the needs and desires of the British Empire. Those needs, access to markets, freedom of trade across international boundaries, an orderly state system that prefers peace to war, speedy communication and travel across open seas and skies remain the principal features of globalization today.

> Of course a complicated historical development on this scale demands far more players and factors than just the British navy. But take it out of the picture and the history of globalization becomes murkier, more haphazard, less inevitable and uncertain. Without out it, a British Empire would have been unthinkable, and without the British Empire and its successor the Commonwealth, half the world's independent nations wouldn't exist today. Other nations might have built a modern unified world, but they probably wouldn't have done it as quickly, efficiently, elegantly, or as humanely. In fact, not since the Roman legions has an ostensibly military force had so decisive an impact on the history of its own nation and the world.
>
> An American, Captain Alfred Mahan was the first to assert that the history of Western civilization has been the history of sea power, the ability of states and empires to exert control over the wide common of the ocean and deny it to others. Through sea power, even a small nation could dominate its neighbours by controlling their access to resources while securing its own and even a small nation could bend events, trends, geography, the globe itself, to its will. This is the essence of 'what it means to rule the waves.'[9]

The British began with a paltry fleet in the fifteenth century that could not have disturbed even a fraction of the European continental fleets, to defeating the Spanish Armada (with the help of a storm sent by God) in 1588 before it could reach the English coast. Once England and Great Britain as a whole realized their innate advantage as an island nation guarded by its "moat defensive,"[10] they dedicated themselves to

9 Arthur Herman. To Rule The Waves. p. xvii

10 Shakespeare, William. Richard II 2.1.48

their naval effort with their hearts and souls. From the early modern era onward, despite their initial disadvantages in land, resources and population, the British increased their sea power until they were the unquestioned masters of the world's oceans, a position they would hold for nearly a century and a half, from the days of Lord Horatio Nelson to Sir Winston Churchill.

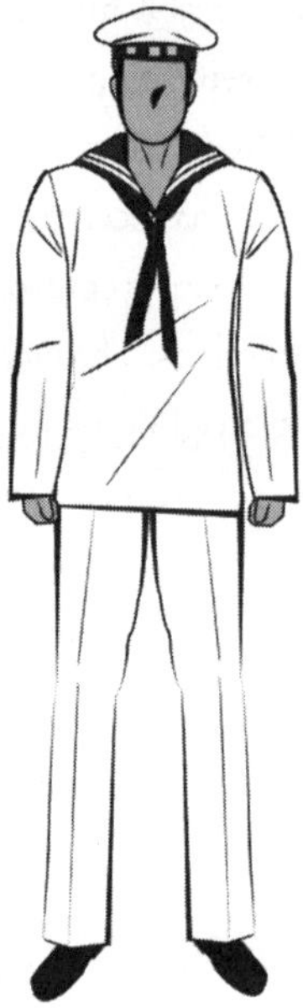

The uniform of the British sailor evolved along with its technology and culture. Eventually the navies of both the American and British fleets would be seen sporting variations of the above uniform. It would go down in history as the modern style of the navy and projected a neat, one might even say, cute image without losing its core ideas of resilience and toughness. It was a masterful stroke of fusing style and fashion with the international navy brand.

Admiral Nelson

Viscount Nelson of the Nile and Burnham Thorpe, also called (1797–98) Sir Horatio Nelson, or (1798–1801) Baron Nelson of the Nile and Burnham Thorpe, (born Sept. 29, 1758, Burnham Thorpe, Norfolk, Eng.—died Oct. 21, 1805, at sea, off Cape Trafalgar, Spain), British naval commander in the wars with Revolutionary and Napoleonic France, who won crucial victories in such battles as those of the Nile (1798) and of Trafalgar (1805), where he was killed by enemy fire on the HMS Victory. In private life he was known for his extended love affair with Emma, Lady Hamilton, while both were married(Encyclopedia Britannica).

Admiral Horatio Nelson was an amazing man with a tenacity and bravery that was unparalleled in his day. He has gone down in history as one of the greatest sea captains of all time; in any country, in any period. His life was not without controversy however, as his stubbornness, flair for the dramatic, torrid romantic relationships and fierce pride provided a sideshow to his spectacular naval career. Even so, whatever you say of his character, what cannot be denied is that Nelson was born to be a great commander. With unwavering confidence and incredible bravery he led the British fleet to victory after victory, insisting on being directly involved in combat until he lost an arm and then was mortally wounded for his trouble, His presence prevented Napoleon's extra-continental ambitions from being realized and set the tone for a century of unquestioned British superiority at sea.

Admiral Nelson atop his pedestal in the aptly named Trafalgar Square maintaining his eternal vigil, daring the French and any other foreign invaders to attempt a channel crossing while the British Royal Navy patrols its waters.

The Legacy

Many important figures are mentioned in this book as heroic (or villainous) representatives of British or American culture, but even among that long list of great people, Horatio Nelson stands out.

He was so deeply revered by his countrymen and his impact was so profound that a century after his death the officers in the British Imperial Navy insisted on using the flag signals he helped innovate, despite the availability of radio communications.[11] When steam powered steel ships were invented, prototypes included sails and many senior navy staff officers doubted their ability to replace the solid oak of Nelson's ships of the line. Nelson became Great Britain's invincible patron god of the sea. However, as impressive as his actual victories were, the myth of the unstoppable Imperial Navy that he helped create was to be an even greater legacy as other seafaring nations backed down from challenging British sea supremacy based on its reputation alone for decades to come. The British now far outnumbered all the other nations' fleets by far, but more than that their naval prowess had taken on a legendary dimension that intimidated other navies into acquiescence. In the short term this Nelson effect was a great blessing, but stubborn dedication to his legacy would eventually begin to slow progress and prevent the acceptance of new innovative approaches. The shadow this man cast over the strategy, technology and tactics of the admiralty was immense and enduring, but there is another aspect of his life that had immeasurable effect, but luckily it did not cause the destruction of the British Imperial Royal Grand Fleet. He

11 This stubborn adherence to naval tradition nearly caused disaster during the Battle of Jutland fought between the British Imperial Navy Royal Grand Fleet and the Imperial German Navy High Seas Fleet from May 31, 1916- June 1, 1916

personally led by example and lost an arm by repeatedly risking his life by maneuvering his ship into close range against his enemies to inflict maximum damage. He risked his life without reservation and thousands upon thousands of sailors followed his example. This is what elevated him in the eyes of his contemporaries, his inspiring presence.

Thus it was that as brilliant as he was tactically, a thing for which he was admired and envied by everyone, to some it was his unshakeable commitment, determination and bravery that mattered most. Ultimately, he was victorious in defeating Napoleon's fleet and ending the threat to the United Kingdom and his charisma, aura of command and supreme confidence played a significant role in that. Among the British and Americans perhaps only George Washington can boast the same leadership quality. He could compel men to follow orders if had to, but often they would suffer and face fear and danger voluntarily, as he would suffer along with them. His men believed in him wholeheartedly at an almost spiritual level and there is no better way to illustrate the complete infatuation and devotion his men had for him then by relating the following anecdote about the origin of the expression "to tap the Admiral"

After expiring from a bullet wound inflicted by a French sniper at the Battle of Trafalgar (1805), Lord Admiral Horatio Nelson was surrounded by a mournful group of staff officers as they brought him below decks on his flagship the HMS Victory. The news of his death was kept secret until the battle's conclusion on his own orders, in order that the morale of the men was not affected. In order to preserve the body, it was placed in a rum cask for the return voyage to England, as the alcohol would prevent decay. The sailors celebrated, drank and toasted their victory and their fallen hero as they sailed homeward. Upon arrival the corpse was taken from the cask and placed into a casket in preparation from an unprecedented funeral procession that would see some of the largest crowds assembled in British history.

While this respectful and formal event was going on, it was whispered that when Nelson's body had been carefully taken from its alcohol filled the container, which had been nearly full at the outset, the cask was drained of its contents! Evidently the sailors, in memorializing their great leader's sacrifice, began imbibing the liquor that was literally infused with his essence. This was done as a tribute and perhaps as a means of staying in contact with him just a little longer and to gain something of his spiritual strength by doing so. Hence the phrase, "to tap the Admiral." A toast to the man who dashed Napoleon's hopes of conquering Britain, with a legacy unlikely to ever be surpassed.

Post-Napoleon Pax Britannica

The Pax Britannica was so named because of the Pax Romana that settled over European in ancient times when the Roman Empire was reigning basically unchallenged over the continent. The term was used to describe the British peace that lasted from 1815 (the end of the

Napoleonic wars) to the outbreak of World War One in August 1914. For roughly a century the British Empire exerted its hegemony over the globe with its world police, much as the Americans do now (which is sometimes also referred to as Pax Americana):

Britain's Royal Navy controlled most of the key maritime trade routes and enjoyed unchallenged sea power. Alongside the formal control it exerted over its own colonies, Britain's dominant position in world trade meant that it effectively controlled access to many regions, such as Asia and Latin America. British merchants, shippers and bankers had such an overwhelming advantage over everyone else that in addition to its colonies it had an "informal empire" (Encyclopedia Britannica).

Dickensian

There has been a great tradition of studying the English literary cannon, a catalogue of classics which are seen to be of the highest quality that deserve meticulous and repeated examination. While some may argue that this approach to education and culture is overdone, there are timeless elements present in certain works of fiction that connect to both the culture of their day and the human condition. One author who was able of accomplishing both these feats was Charles Dickens. Writing in the mid-19th century, he was an incredibly prolific writer who produced new stories almost by the week. His most famous works such as *Oliver Twist, A Tale of Two Cities* and *A Christmas Carol*, as much as his lesser known works, resonated with the British populace as he created compelling characters dealing with the realities of the Industrial Revolution, moral questions related to religion, manners, class, children and more. His short stories were purchased by the hundreds of thousands at a half-penny each. His readership was larger than any previous author and reached audiences across Victorian England in a way never seen before. His influence and style were so profound that when a situation, event, story or behavior seems reminiscent of him it is called; Dickensian.

Her Life and Her Letters

In contrast to the previous author, some people are more easily passed over, or so it would seem. Passing over people happens to be the main result of any broad examination of culture, and of history to boot and so the Dickens and Shakespeares stand out. Only a fraction of humanity has left a legacy for us to study; much has been lost through accident. However, there are times when individuals who are suppressed, ignored or shunted aside find a way to make an immense contribution to our culture. Their impact reverberates across society and leaves a mark just as a medieval king might. Whole sections of society have been left out of histories, and women have often been included among them. With notable exceptions, few remarkable women appear before the modern era, and even then they are not brought to the forefront as influential players. This is not a coincidence or an accident, as an entire patriarchal system has dominated British and American culture since the beginning of recorded history. Thus, it is essential that we discuss women that are representative of this talent, desire, ambition and insistence in having a voice. Even more significant, the women who took it upon themselves, despite their circumstances, to express themselves and make themselves heard. Jane Austen was one of these women.

Austen was born in 1776, a fortuitous year for America and less so for the British. She was raised in England, where she attended a boarding school for girls, got married and settled down to a life of complicated society in the English countryside. Just like the characters in her famous books *Pride and Prejudice* and *Sense and Sensibility*, which are among her six most famous novels. Debate continues about whether Jane had to hide her manuscripts, she was shy or that she simply published her books anonymously as many others did. What is not debatable is the quality of the writing, and the fact that she was a woman in a published world dominated by men. Within the intricacies of the social circles, manners, humour and vivid characters, there lies a critique of the world of the gentleman that would seem to reflect her own reality. On multiple levels her readers could share Jane's experience of that society, whether partially true, or imagined. Women may identify with the Austen world, but the cultural experience she proffered has been attractive and informative to all genders.

She was, in some sense, like Shakespeare; who some people believe did not write his own plays because of his lower class status, humble background and grammar school education. After all, how could a boy from Stratford rise to become the master bard? In fact, Jane Austen had additional limitations; being a girl who was expected to mind her place in society, and not challenge the status quo, but we have ample evidence that she penned the works that have also been elevated the hallowed literary canon posthumously, as were his. Perhaps she proves Shakespeare's case, perhaps not, but for women she proves their equal capability and potential in the literary field, and British culture in particular owes her a debt of gratitude; for this is another essential part of the British and American identity: the development of an increasing, more dynamic, more important role for women in society. A point of view that would complicate the vision of society in the Victorian era and ever after; in a good way. After all, where would the Woolfs or Rowlings be without Austen?

Queen Victoria

Victoria, in full Alexandrina Victoria, (born May 24, 1819, Kensington Palace, London, England—died January 22, 1901, Osborne, near Cowes, Isle of Wight), queen of the United Kingdom of Great Britain and Ireland (1837–1901) and empress of India (1876–1901). She was the last of the house of Hanover and gave her name to an era, the Victorian Age. During her reign the British monarchy took on its modern ceremonial character. She and her husband, Prince Consort Albert of Saxe-Coburg-Gotha, had nine children, through whose marriages were descended many of the royal families of Europe.

Victoria first learned of her future role as a young princess during a history lesson when she was 10 years old. Almost four decades later Victoria's governess recalled that the future queen reacted to the discovery by declaring, "I will be good." This combination of earnestness and egotism marked Victoria as a child of the age that bears her name. The queen, however, rejected important Victorian values and developments. Although she hated pregnancy and childbirth, detested babies, and was uncomfortable in the presence of children, Victoria reigned in a society that idealized both motherhood and the family. She had no interest in social issues, yet the 19th century in Britain was an age of reform. She resisted technological change even while mechanical and technological innovations reshaped the face of European civilization.

Most significantly, Victoria was a queen determined to retain political power, yet unwillingly and unwittingly she presided over the transformation of the sovereign's political role into a ceremonial one and thus preserved the British monarchy. When Victoria became queen, the political role of the crown was by no means clear; nor was the permanence of the throne itself. When she died and her son Edward VII moved from Marlborough House to Buckingham Palace, the change was one of social rather than of political focus; there was no doubt about the monarchy's continuance. That was the measure of her reign (Encyclopedia Britannica).

Victoria, like her predecessor Queen Elizabeth I, ended up ruling alone. After her husband Prince Albert passed away she receded into her own bubble and appeared less than jovial when in public. Her serious exterior, conservative policies and pious behaviour set the tone for much of the imperial age. The dress, manners, art, literature and architecture of the 19thcentury is still known as Victorian. Though she wielded little actual political and imperial power, her influence on official policy and the public was undeniable. Her diamond jubilee was both a celebration of her longevity and a testament to imperial British success at the height of its potency. Not only did she spread her influence domestically and throughout the empire, but many of her children also married into the royal families of Europe making her the most connected woman on Earth. There is hardly an aspect of British culture that was not touched by Queen Victoria and so her place in its evolution is guaranteed forever.

Across the Pond in the 19th Century America

While the British Empire continued to expand, Charles Dickens penned his famous novels and Queen Victoria continued her record-breaking reign as a female monarch, the growth in the United States continued to accelerate. As the states multiplied and territories expanded, the political differences of the ante-bellum period inevitably came to a head in the American Civil War. After the Union victory and the re-absorption of the South, the Reconstruction period began in order to both rebuild the physical damage to the South and to heal political divisions, cultural divisions and racial tensions. This task proved too much for the new administration to handle as the South relapsed into a segregated society where slavery was illegal and former black slaves' (as well as other minorities) rights were guaranteed federally, but non-existent locally.

Simultaneously, there was a burst of industriousness, innovation and westward expansion. The transportation revolution was well under way as canals were dug connecting lakes, rivers and oceans, while railroads began to crisscross the vastness of America linking farms, towns, villages and cities. These transportation networks penetrated into the interior and even farther west, allowing settling, farming, resource extraction and exploration of an entire continent. Huge corporations producing oil, steel, ships and other commodities made people fabulously wealthy. It was the age of the 'robber barons,' the tycoons of the 19th century. And while some of the most famous of these men; Andrew Carnegie and John D. Rockefeller, did donate enormous amounts of money in their latter years in generous acts of philanthropy, their cutthroat business strategies, relentless acquisition and pursuit of profit created immense wealth at the top, while many among the masses suffered and did without. Thus, this period has come to be known as the Gilded Age. If placed alongside with the labels the post-bellum period, the Reconstruction Era, it describes the last three decades from vastly different social, political and cultural experiences.

The Father of American Literature

We would be remiss, if the man who some have called the 'Father of American Literature,' Mark Twain, was not introduced in the course of this book. Just as Austen and Dickens were able to use their writing to capture a cultural moment in England, Mark Twain was able to communicate ideas, philosophies, and experiences from the viewpoint of a child. His stories dealt with freedom, racism, child abuse, greed, justice and many other themes that called into question the perceived American prosperity of the late 19th century. It is important also to understand that though he was an anti-imperialist and an abolitionist, he would not seem progressive by today's standards, but in this case it is essential that one looks at the relative progress his literature and his personal efforts pushed forward. Despite being criticized for dumbing down the language in his most famous works *The Adventures of Tom Sawyer* and *Adventures of Huckleberry Finn*, his insistence on writing dialogues that were true to regional dialects, accents, mispronunciations, incorrect grammar and uneducated characters, were soon accepted as more realistic and resulted in the timeless naughty rebellious characters that remain popular to this day. His chosen optics did much to re-align his readers' perception that the impressive wealth and prestige of the great politicians and industrialists, there amazing achievements in production, technology and trade, were largely out of touch and with the majority of the American people. Again, many 21st century individuals would see him as not taking his ideas far enough, but for most of his life his was very active in promoting civil rights and remains a respected individual for those efforts.

British and American Culture:
Evolution and Revolution

Chapter **07**

Twentieth Century Boy

Chapter 07 Twentieth Century Boy

Modernism, Art & the Seminal Tragedy

The word modern has now become synonymous with progress, newness, and advancement. Modernists attempt to break from the past by emphasizing individuality, speed and forward momentum. It also encouraged a belief in the human ability to control, create and improve all aspects of life took hold in many cultures. British and American culture were no exception. Furthermore, if we were to examine particular literary examples of Modernism, James Joyce, Virgina Woolf, T.S Eliot and Ernest Hemingway would provide a good sampling of its features. Their use of stream of consciousness, realism, symbolism, and memory in their poems, short stories and novels have revealed more about society, gender, individuality and the human condition as our understanding of the universe, the world and civilization expands. Additionally, great artists like Van Gogh, Monet, Picasso and Dali simultaneously transformed the art world with their abstract visions, but no British or American Painters are among those masters. The Industrial and Scientific Revolutions had put new tools and machines in the hands of people, giving them unprecedented power over nature. Modernism also affected literature, society, politics and art, but here our object is to discuss the direct consequences on the loss of human life when an unbridled faith in human progress takes hold. Modernism began an unprecedented organization of people, a rapid development of new technologies that harnessed industrial power, improved transportation networks and new mass communication systems as a means for making total war.

Most of the concepts that underlie modernism are still present in our society today, but with the sobering thought and tempered knowledge of the potential for catastrophic consequences. The Great War (now known as World War One), was that moment when military culture, technology, society and politics collided. The result was a disaster that has only been matched by its even more destructive sequel; World War Two.

In many ways this war was the most remarkable transition in the history of military warfare and global culture. A simple analysis of the types of units, equipment, weapons, machines, tactics, politics, attitudes and public opinions that shifted from 1914-1918 reveals how dramatic the European, if not the whole world, had changed. Empires were shattered, broken and re-constituted. Governments rose and fell, territories exchanged hands. Tanks were invented, airplanes were adapted for aerial combat, submarines entered the fray, alliances were formed, treaties were ignored, atrocities and war crimes committed, radios and radar provided information on the enemy, the home front mass-produced war materiel, massive loans were undertaken to fund the war effort, and that is not nearly all. The concept of total war, on an industrial scale had taken human conflict to a different level, and the world would never be the same. No longer would war be glorious, with heroes impressing their countrymen and coming home to their families, their loved ones and admirers. War was hell. It had become a monstrous and dehumanizing experience that left physical and psychological scars on all the participants. Thousands of British and American soldiers returned home with terrible wounds, missing legs arms, burned faces, lungs damaged by mustard gas. For the British it was the most injurious and damaging war in their history, not just in terms of money, property or casualties, but also in prestige. A generation of men laid down their lives for the Empire, which was saved, but it would soon begin to slowly deflate, "like a flan in a cupboard."[1] America for its part would escape the worst of the structural damage and suffer less casualties, while its

1 Izzard, Eddie.

economy was humming due to wartime demand, but it would not be long before the hollow victory in achieving Germany's surrender were erased by the Great Depression and the rise of Nazism in Hitler's Third Reich.

The New Britannia - Goodbye to the Empire Where the Sun Never Sets

There is a great deal of nostalgia when it comes to Great Britain's history and that feeling is in part derived from a feeling that its greatest days are past. Even before the gradual dismantling of the Empire, British citizens were lamenting its loss. The process was begun even as the British Empire reached its zenith going into the twentieth century. Has it been all downhill from then? Was the 'soft landing' from empire back to a regional national power a mortal blow to British pride, and a permanent change in its culture? The results are still not out on that subject, but there is no shortage of opinions:

> Intellectually, the Whig saga was moribund. The Cambridge historian Herbert Butterfield (later Master of Peterhouse) wrote a pugnacious pamphlet, *The Whig Interpretation of History* (1931), condemning it as a "caricature" of the past pandering to the "ideas and prejudices" of the present. A real caricature had appeared a year before Butterfield's manifesto, 1066 and All That, by W.C. Sellar and R.J Yeatman, which made Butterfield's point more amusingly and to a vastly wider readership: almost every episode in history was "a Good

Thing" as it advanced Britain's progress to "Top Nation."[2]

A preoccupation with "what has gone wrong with England" gave a body blow to Whig history as the national narrative. It had been a history of success: that is why the American version outlives the British original. It had shown England and its overseas offshoots as leading the world towards freedom, the rule of law and representative government. The First World War shook such confidence. The Second provided a last defiant flourish—Butterfield even wrote that it had made the myth true—but the postwar torrent of "declinism"... gave the coup de grâce. The end of empire and the spread of democracy ended British exceptionalism. The successes of recently democratized states such as Germany negated the idea that long historical experience was a source of unique political wisdom. The prestige of ancient institutions—now often presented as embarrassingly archaic and ripe for "modernization"—towards alignment with Continental norms. Anti-establishment historians could now recast the Whig story of centuries of noble political struggle ending in triumph into one of bitter class conflict ending in failure.[3]

The Emergence of a New American Identity

Meanwhile across the pond (the Atlantic Ocean) a sort of American imperialism began to take hold. It was perceived that the United States had now earned its place among the great powers of the world and, much like Germany, it felt it deserved the same privileges. This included colonies, overseas territories and a navy to support them.

2 Robert Toombs. The English and Their History. p. 271-272

3 Robert Toombs. The English and Their History. p. 272-273

However, this rising movement had a fundamental flaw to overcome; it was inherently and directly contradictory to the spirit that drove the Revolutionary War and the creation of the republic. America had fought against the tyranny of empire to gain its freedom in the first place. Furthermore, it was George Washington himself that declared America would remain neutral and not become entangled in foreign politics. Obviously, the opinion of the first President carried some weight, but this new aggressive 'jingoist' faction steadily moved public opinion. One of the chief proponents of a more aggressive foreign policy was Theodore Roosevelt, who would eventually get his way as America expanded overseas and entered World War One on the side of the allies. The dichotomy of war and peace, isolationism and expansionism, neutrality and intervention would continue, but this era would mark the beginning of the evolution into a hyper-interventionalist state. Howard Zinn describes how pivotal the Spanish-American War in the 1890s was to American culture in this respect:

> War and jingoism might postpone, but could not fully suppress, the class anger that came from the realities of ordinary life. As the twentieth century opened, that anger re-emerged. Emma Goldman, the anarchist and feminist, who political consciousness was shaped by factory work, the Haymarket executions, the Homestead strike, the long prison term of her lover and comrade, Alexander Berkman, the depression of the 1890s, the strike struggle of New York, her own

imprisonment on Blackwell's Island, spoke at a meeting some years after the Spanish-American war:

> How our hearts burned with indignation against the atrocious Spaniards!... But when the smoke was over, the dead buried, and the cost of the war came back to the people in an increase in the price of commodities and rent—
>
> That is, when we sobered up from our patriotic spree—it suddenly dawmed on us that the cause of the Spanish-American war was the price of sugar... that the lives, blood, and money of the American people were used to protect the interests of American capitalists.[4]

Entering the modern era: The American Century

At the beginning of the twentieth century it was plain to see that two nations were on the rapid rise, Russia and the United States of America. Culturally and historically they were immensely different, but they had at least one thing in common, rapidly expanding land-based territories that were approaching their limits. What would happen when these two super powers expanded far enough that they encountered each other in regions besides the unpopulated, frozen seas of the Bering Strait? As it turned out, the Cold War would happen, but the Russians would be outlasted by the Americans and they would coin it their century, rather than the Russians:

> It was Henry Luce, the founder of Time, who in a signed editorial

4 Howard Zinn. A People's History of the United States. p. 321

in his own magazine made popular the phrase "the American Century." The century was then already more than two-fifths over. It was 1941, and the Japanese had not yet attacked Pearl Harbor. The argument rumbled on whether the United States should enter the war on the side of Britain against Japanese militarism and German and Italian fascism, as President Franklin Delano Roosevelt privately thought inevitable, or should remain neutral, as a majority of both Congress and public opinion still preferred.

Luce wrote of the American Century not out of triumphalist nationalism but as a prophet calling on his countrymen to take up a burden in the spirit of Christian sacrifice. America should save Britain, Luce said, but, more than that, "we must undertake now to be the Good Samaritan of the entire world." He saw his country as destined to lift mankind "from the level of the beasts to what the Psalmist called a little lower than the angels." The history of the rest of the American century can be seen as a commentary on the extent to which Luce's countrymen lived up to his vision, at home and abroad.[5]

Early Optimism in the 1910s

So how did this momentum all get started and whatever happened to the British Empire in all this? The answer to that is exceedingly complex, but the long and the short of it is that the age of empires came to a rapid end as the powder keg that was European diplomatic alliances at the beginning of the twentieth century exploded into a world war, which was originally named the "Great War," right up until another

5 Godfrey Hodgson. The Cambridge Companion to Modern American Culture. p. 33

world war broke out 20 years later. While America emerged out of a deep recession and its economy strengthened, the astronomical cost of the war effort plunged the European combatants into debt. Going into 1914 Great Britain was still the leading global economic and sea power, but the pivot to North America, especially economically, was abrupt and America was pulling ahead by the 1920s.

WWI (The Great War)

It was much easier for America to be positive about the war in Europe when it was profiting by selling goods and equipment to both sides. When it finally did enter the war it was to join the allies in their final pushes against an exhausted German military and a fragmenting, collapsing Austro-Hungarian Empire. The American state got the economic benefit from the incredible industrial production of the war effort, while simultaneously getting credit for the final victory and taking minimal losses in doing so:

> "War is the health of the state," the radical writer Randolph Bourne said, in the midst of the First World War. Indeed, as the nations of Europe went to war in 1914, the governments flourished, patriotism bloomed, class struggle was stilled, and young men died in frightful numbers on the battlefields—often for a hundred yards of land, a line of trenches.
>
> In the United States, not yet in the war, there was worry about the health of the state. Socialism was growing. The IWW seemed to be everywhere. Class conflict was intense. In the summer of 1916, during

a Preparedness Day parade in San Francisco, a bomb exploded, killing nine people; two local radicals, Tom Mooney and Warren Billings, were arrested and would spend twenty years in prison. Shortly after that Senator James Wadsworth of New York suggested compulsory military training for all males to avert the danger that "these people of ours shall be divided into classes." Rather: "We must let our young men know that they owe some responsibility to this country."[6]

The Great Depression

At the end of the 1920s the incredible bull run that had driven the biggest stock exchange in the world to new heights had run its course. First the London Stock Exchange was rocked by a crash and that was followed less than a month later by a corresponding, more serious and deeper crash in the NYSE (New York Stock Exchange). The fundamentals that had driven economic development and the over-optimistic investment of the previous decade suddenly vanished leaving the majority of banks and many companies illiquid and insolvent. The money dried up so fast that many people could not even withdraw their savings. Bankruptcies and home foreclosures quickly numbered in the thousands, while unemployment skyrocketed. The British economy crumbled along with the American as nearly one in three people were soon out of work. A global crisis ensued and governments were at a loss as to how to solve the problem. The stage was set for revolution in many countries as the social pressure was too much to bear.

6 Howard Zinn. A People's History of the United States.p.359.

Into this crisis came one of the most famous Americans of the modern era, President Franklin Delano Roosevelt (FDR). He proposed a "New Deal" of public spending on infrastructure that would help lift the American economy out of the doldrums and put it back on the sure footing of the previous decade. His program was successful to some degree, but it paled in comparison to the success of his counterpart in Germany Adolf Hitler, who had miraculously turned the seemingly hopeless and endless recessions of the German state into an economic success story. It was later revealed that a massive military industrial build up was the main reason for this amazing success, and it would require a similar military build up for the United States to truly break free of its own deep recession years by developing its own military-industrial complex that maximized war-time production and the employment of both men and women on the home front. Military equipment, vehicles and research would propel the United States to victory in Europe and the Pacific, while at the same time claiming a massive part of government spending and providing economic growth for the next three quarters of a century.

Military vehicles such as this tank parked in an open lot were an essential part of the British and the American army in World War Two. Production of these vehicles required design, research, material, resources, fuel, transportation and above all labor to be put in the field. Huge numbers of people were employed in the effort to get military vehicles off the line at home and into action on the front line.

WW2 and the Liberal Consensus

World War Two saw the United States again engaged in a war overseas which it was somewhat reluctant to be drawn into, but after the Japanese surprise attack and the German declaration of war, the majority of the nation was convinced of the necessity. America was now visibly evolving into the interventionist world policing entity that people of the twenty-first century are so familiar with.

The massive mobilization and increased industrial capacity that followed those declarations of war caused an economic boom that would carry America forward for several decades. Prosperity in the middle class was at a level never before seen in modern society, and has rarely been rivaled in all of Western history. The destruction of Europe was also unequaled in the modern era as it surpassed even the devastation of World War I, so America stood virtually alone atop the globe for a time. However, the lessons of the interim years between the two World Wars were well taken and a bipartisan consensus was formed based around the rebuilding and recovery of the nations damaged in the global conflict. Among the many assistance programs were loans, subsidies and most famously the "Marshall Plan". The culture of the United States would spread across the world on an unprecedented scale. Godfrey Hodgson explains how this occurred in his paper aptly titled *The American Century*:

> The American economy was badly damaged by the Great Depression. But when war came again, once again the territory and industry of the United States were untouched. The economy was revived again by the war orders before Pearl Harbor and the prodigious effort to build American military power between 1942 and 1945. When the conflict ended American industry, with for a time no competitors, enjoyed monopoly profits.
>
> The immediate postwar years were a time not just of great prosperity but of wealth more equitably distributed than any time since the United States first began to industrialize after the Civil War. With strong government controls and a major role for government in investment, development, and research, it was a social democratic boom. For the first time, millions of Americans bought their own homes... Unions collaborated with corporate management.

> Unemployment was low, real wages grew rapidly, and there was massive investment in housing, industrial plant[s], and transport. This was the age of the "liberal consensus"" conservatives, more or less reluctantly, accepted the domestic welfare state, while liberals – admittedly with significant exceptions on the Left – accepted the anti-communist foreign policy of the Right.[7]

The British Were There Too

In all the flag-waving and victory achieving that came along with the American entrance in both World Wars it is easy to forget who bore the brunt of the aggression. In both cases the answer is fairly clear: France, Great Britain and Russia. Who ultimately delivered the allied victory? That is less clear, but ultimately most historians would argue: World War One, France; World War Two; Russia. So why does the United States get all the credit? The answer to that is rather simple, they emerged with their territory virtually unscathed and their borders intact after both global conflicts, making them the clear winners in both wars (along with Japan in the First World World War) because they suffered comparatively few losses. For Great Britain however, the First World War was incredibly devastating in terms of casualties and economic cost; it faced a lot more adversity and had a lot more to overcome. Also, let us not forget that at one point there was only one nation left standing to stop the Nazi war machine; the United Kingdom of Great Britain.

7 Godfrey Hodgson. The Cambridge Companion to Modern American Culture. p. 37.

British Determination

Sir Winston Churchill is a perfect example of the enduring presence of the British. British power has now waned from its peak in the late 19th century, but still persists as a general echo of British power across the globe. The prestige of the British Empire and the insistence of its preeminent position have been of inestimable political and strategic value. From trade, to security, to education, to diplomacy and perhaps most importantly, in war, their reputation has served the well. Churchill was in essence an imperialist, a member of the "old guard," who still believed that it was the destiny of Great Britain to continue to be a world leader and he would maintain this conviction, even to the grave. His oratory skills, his political savviness and bulldog stubbornness went down in history as the United Kingdom briefly stood alone facing Nazi Germany, as it had faced down Napoleon. Churchill did not back down from the challenge, confident as he was in the capacity of the British nation to handle the crisis.

On the other hand, there has long been a camp of British politicians, intellectuals and historians that have decried the decline of British power. In some circles this is seen as a product of "Whig history" which sees British history as a forward march of progress than reached its apex in the formation of the constitutional government and in the maximum extent of British territorial and cultural influence. To their eye Britain has been in terminal decline since the late 19th century. Even before it reached its economic and territorial heights in the Victorian era, the decline of Britain was already being lamented. However, the strength of the British brand still persists, the pound is still the most valuable currency in the world[8] and the people continue to carry the torch passed on from Churchill still believe in the muscularity of British culture.

Winston Churchill was a controversial figure in his own time, but his charisma, obstinacy and poise in Britain's dire time of need has left him with a legacy that is almost unparalleled. Standing virtually alone against the advancing Nazi forces of Adolf Hitler in 1940, he delivered eloquent speeches and inspiring words to a British state on the brink of disaster. He is remembered fondly despite his many faults and missteps. He continues to be a great symbol of Britishness and has had an enduring effect on British culture.

8 Among fiat(official) currency (Bitcoin and other cryptocurriencies being excepted of course)

A Continuum of Contradictions

The stage was set for the Cold War as soon as World War Two ended. The maps were divided in two wherever the two remaining super powers met. Countries were literally split in half by the Russians and Americans, as in the cases of Korea and Germany. All across the globe there were zones of potential conflict where World War Three might break out at any moment. The American air and sea superiority were countered by the Red Army's terrifyingly immense army and land superiority with its tens of thousands of tanks ready to steamroll right to the Atlantic coast from the eastern bloc; if given the order. It was a classic military stalemate even before the mutually assured destructive power of nuclear tipped intercontinental ballistic missiles (ICBMs) entered the picture. An international standoff ensued for next five decades:

> The creation of the United Nations at the conclusion of the war was presented to the world as international cooperation to prevent future wars. But the U.N. was dominated by the Western imperial countries—the United States, England, and France—and a new imperial power, with military bases and powerful influence in Eastern Europe—the Soviet Union.[9]

9 Howard Zinn. A People's History of the United States. p.415

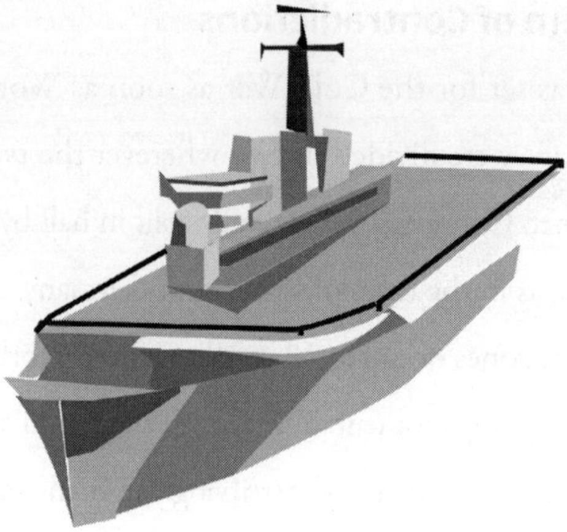

Civil Rights

With the post-war boom subsiding and the success of the global economic recovery, unrest began to spread in the 1960s. Americans had gained so much, but many were still excluded from sharing the wealth of the states and from participating as equal citizens. This unrest would gain momentum and snowball into the American Civil Rights Movement.

The Civil Rights Movement was an explosion of social disapproval at the entrenched inequality and discriminatory practices against different races, genders, sexualities, religions, classes and professions, among others in America. Across the country a wide variety of groups expressed solidarity by protesting together against the lack of government support for or protection of human rights. There were particularly charismatic individuals who drove this movement, such as Martin Luther King, who was assassinated for his role in leading the

African-American movement. The accomplishments of the protesters were myriad and they resulted in a number of laws being passed that protected the rights and freedoms of all American citizens no matter their background or appearance. However, the following is a startling example of irrational segregation practices that only served to hurt individuals and society, that occurred leading up to the movement and why it needed to occur:

> The Red Cross, with government approval, separated the blood donations of black and white. It was, ironically, a black physician named Charles Drew who developed the blood bank system. He was put in charge of the wartime donations, and then fired when he tried to end blood segregation. Despite the urgent need for wartime labor, blacks were still being discriminated against for jobs. A spokesperson for a West Coast aviation plant said: "The Negro will be considered only as janitors and in other similar capacities... Regardless of their training as aircraft workers, we will not employ them." Roosevelt never did anything to enforce the orders of the Fair Employment Practices Commission he set up.[10]

Neo-Cons and the New Bi-partisan Consensus

In a way the final era of the American century was a response to the liberally driven protests of the 60s and has been dominated by new conservative politics. Having achieved so much and evolved into a country that was the envy of the world, it was time for America

10 Howard Zinn. A People's History of the United States. p.415

to kick back and consolidate. So what happens to a country and a culture that is propelled to the top and then sits aloof without serious competition or necessity driving it to improve, progress or better itself? Intellectuals of all kinds going back to the days of the ancient Greeks and Romans have wondered about this question. Is it part of the life cycle of a civilization to be tough on the rise and to go soft on the way down? Does competition and adversity force a culture to produce tougher more capable individuals as well as forcing people to be "better" and more reasonable? These questions are difficult to answer, but it seems that most Americans would not argue that the quality of each generation has declined since the so-called "greatest generation" endured the Great Depression and then won World War Two. The liberal consensus was an agreement on the necessity to rebuild a shattered global economy and the Civil Rights Movement drove social change in a revolution born out of protest, but what of the last era of the American century? Arguably it has continued into the twentieth century as a stagnant carryover of failed American foreign policy and an attempt to preserve the American ascendancy. After such disasters as the Vietnam War, the Iraqi War and Afghanistan among others over the last few decades, should policy not change? Whether it is argued that the system is broken, that America is stuck in a rut or that nothing has forced change in a society that continues to float on its past successes, the warning signs appeared long ago, but the bi-partisan consensus on foreign policy remains unchanged:

Halfway through the twentieth century, the historian Richard Hofstadter, in his book *The American Political Tradition*, examined our important national leaders, from Jefferson to Herbert Hoover and the two Roosevelts—Republicans and Democrats, liberals and conservatives. Hofstadter concluded that "the range of vision embraced by the primary contestants in the major parties has always been bounded by the horizons of property and enterprise... They have accepted the economic virtues of capitalist culture as necessary qualities of man... That culture has been intensely nationalistic..."

Coming to the end of the [twentieth century], observing its last twenty-five years, we have seen exactly that limited vision Hofstadter talked about—a capitalistic encouragement of enormous fortunes alongside desperate poverty, a nationalistic acceptance of war and preparations for war. Governmental power swung from Republicans to Democrats and back again, but neither party showed itself capable of going beyond that vision.

After the disastrous war in Vietnam came the scandals of Watergate. There was a deepening economic insecurity for much of the population, along with environmental deterioration, and a growing culture of violence and family disarray. Clearly, such fundamental problems could not be solved without bold changes in the social and economic structure. But no major party candidates proposed such changes. The "American political tradition" held fast.[11]

American Cinema

American cinema has stagnated of late, just as the culture of the America has lost some of its zest, but in its heyday it was a truly

11 Howard Zinn. A People's History of the United States. p.563

revolutionary industry. From the constantly evolving technology in the early twentieth century, to the creativity and innovation of the 1960s and 1970s as directors and studios tested new genres and styles, the American film has changed so much its original productions have now become virtually unwatchable. Tragically for the evolution and the diversity of films the rising cost of production and talent coupled with intense competition has given Hollywood a strangle hold on American movies. Now, only a few studios have survived out of an original pool of dozens. This has resulted in the recycling of old successful ideas; namely adaptations, reboots and remakes. Interestingly though, the development of Hollywood is an amazingly accurate reflection of the development of American culture as a whole. The progression of Hollywood over the twentieth century is laid out below. The parallels to the previous discussion on the American century's cultural progress should be obvious as cinematic eras overlap on political and economic eras.

The Black and White Era

Yes, there was no sound! It sounds incredibly boring, black and white, no sound, or special effects, just written dialogue and actors gesturing at each other? But you have to imagine that you had never seen this technology before. People who saw these "shorts" (short films) were actually stunned and in complete awe of them when they were demonstrated. They called them 'moving pictures' and that is how the American fixation with the big screen began. A leap from still pictures to minutes of moving visuals, is like the leap from riding a horse to driving a car and then to flying a plane. American cinematic technology in the early twentieth century would create and then revolutionize an entire industry in the decades to come.

The Classical Hollywood Era

The Classical Hollywood Era witnessed the rise of the film industry to its highest level of popularity. The majority of Americans were visiting the cinema weekly producing record Box Office sales. This had partly to do with the economic and social climate, partly to do with the newness of the technology and partly to do with lack of competition. The result of this increased popularity was higher salaries for actors as studios began to recognize that their fame attracted huge audiences and had them coming back for more. In addition, sound was first added at the beginning of this era and colour towards its end, giving viewers a more realistic movie experience.

The Golden Age

The peak of cinema popularity happened when movies were new and there was no competition, and then it had a resurgence during World War II. There are many reasons for the decline in viewership, but one must assume separation of studios from their monopolies on cinema ownership, or spread of other forms of entertainment as alternatives were the primary factors.

The Decline of the Studio System

Probably the most important factor in the decline of the studio system was the invention of the television. The earliest technology available to the public resembled the T.V. set above, and later models rapidly improved on them. So the proliferation of the technology and the development of a variety of programs, started to audiences into their living rooms and away from the cinema.

New Hollywood

In this era of Hollywood, somewhat confusingly still named "new", directors were to play a more significant role. The period is generally marked from the mid-1960s to the end of the 1980s when new technology and the next generation of filmmakers began to innovate and change the way movies were constructed. The most lasting effect of the New Hollywood era is the larger salaries and creative control that is now given to the marquis directors. In some cases the director's star power again began to rival that of the star actor, enabling them to wield greater creative control.

Contemporary Hollywood

Special effects were the order of the day as Hollywood moved into the Contemporary Hollywood era. During the last few decades expensive technical expertise and equipment have further separated the big studios from the small independents.

With the advent of the internet many assumed assumed sales and movie theater attendance would drop even further, but neither appears to be true. The internet just served to entice audiences to bootleg or watch recorded content later in the same way that home video cassettes did. The internet provided a medium to transmit movies across the world, but also a way to advertise for new audiences to visit the cinema.

Another addition in this era is the late 20th century Hollywood action hero. An invincible macho hypersexual male (or less commonly; an irresistible female) figure of few words that can defeat any villain, no matter how unlikely to scenario. This figure is largely based on the western cowboy hero with some added characteristics. The series "Taken" featuring the actor Liam Neeson, is a great example, as is

Bruce Willis' character John McClane of the Die Hard series, that demonstrates the invincibility of the action hero. On occasion a woman (see Lara Croft played by Angelina Jolie) will fulfill the same role, but the majority of the characters and therefore actors are male. The invincible unbeatable American hero has been reproduced over and over and continues to be perpetuated in the recent twenty-first century superhero craze.

CGI and the Hollywood Blockbuster

A completely artificially generated world is what a CGI film is. As in the movie Avatar where an entire planet was created to drive the magical special effects infused story (a story that was in essence a visually upgraded recycling of the animated movie *Fern Gully* by Disney Pictures). Whatever form they take, Science Fiction, Superhero, Adventure or Action film, Hollywood blockbusters are characteristically big budget films with pre-established marketing and branding already in place. Other examples include The Transformers series, DC Comics or the Marvel series. They are basically internationally guaranteed bestsellers as the fanbase is already there, having grown up reading the comics or watching the cartoons or being exposed to other similar films in the theater beforehand. And so the American cinema sits at the same point as American culture does now; with immense amounts of money being spent on the same production with little competition driving people to be creative or innovative.

The American Presidency

FDR

Franklin D. Roosevelt, byname FDR (born January 30, 1882, Hyde Park, New York, U.S.—died April 12, 1945, Warm Springs, Georgia), 32nd president of the United States (1933–45). The only president elected to the office four times, Roosevelt led the United States through two of the greatest crises of the 20th century: the Great Depression and World War II. In so doing, he greatly expanded the powers of the federal government through a series of programs and reforms known as the New Deal, and he served as the principal architect of the successful effort to rid the world of German National Socialism and Japanese militarism (Encyclopedia Britannica).

Coming onto the political scene in a country that had been coasting along nicely and then crashing to its worst level since the Civil War period, F.D.R. had his work cut out for him. While he has his critics, it is indisputable that this man's guidance, from the New Deal to World War II, won him an unprecedented four terms in office and gives him at least partial credit for the dramatic turnaround in his country while he was President.

Eisenhower

Dwight D. Eisenhower was a natural choice for President after the American public's disillusionment with the Truman administration. It was nearly impossible to fill the gigantic shoes of F.D.R., but if any person was capable, it was this man. He was a well-known gambler, an expert Bridge and Poker player, which made him, along with his military resume, one of the most intimidating Presidents of all-time. You would not want to be caught calling his bluff.

Being one of the most powerful men in the 20th century, Dwight Eisenhower may have taken a demotion when he became the President of the U.S.A when he stepped down at Supreme Allied Commander and head of NATO. He famously warned of the dangers of the military-industrial complex that was created in WW2.

Kennedy

John F. Kennedy was born in 1917 Brookline, Massachusetts and died when he was assassinated while riding in a motorcade in Dallas in 1963. He was 35th president of the United States (1961–63), and faced a number of foreign crises, especially in Cuba and Berlin, but somehow managed to successfully avet a direct confrontation with the Soviet Union that had the potential to start a nuclear war. It has been argued that the danger and the tension during his Presidency had the potential to destroy all civilisation as we know it. It was a unique moment in human history. Thus, his appearance, charismatic speeches and dashing smile should all remain secondary to his geo-political achievements in keeping the world intact.

Unfortunately for President John F. Kennedy his youthful appearance and claims of natural exuberance and natural energy were just a façade. He had some serious medical conditions and was heavily medicated for the last years of his life, including during his Presidency. Despite this, he navigated the country through some of the most tumultuous years of its existence before he was assassinated while parading in his motorcar down a street in Dallas, Texas.

Nixon

Richard Nixon, in full Richard Milhous Nixon was born January 9, 1913, Yorba Linda, California, U.S. He was the 37th president of the United States (1969–74), and when he faced almost certain impeachment for his role in the Watergate scandal, he became the first American president to resign from office. He was also vice president (1953–61) under President Dwight D. Eisenhower (Encyclopedia Britannica).

"I am not a crook!" claimed Richard Nixon to the press.

But he was a crook, and he was caught red-handed, on tape. He resigned rather than be impeached, but it is one of the great embarrassments of the Republican Party in America, the Presidential Office and of the American Government in general. This is why his legacy is forever tarnished and his behavior is a stain on the strong proud American governmental tradition. He has gone down in history as one of the most disliked Presidents, in particular because of his lying and denials after the scandal came to light. Any of his positive contributions tend to be overshadowed by the cover-up and corruption related to his involvement in Watergate.

Reagan

Ronald Reagan was born February 6, 1911, Tampico, Illinois, U.S. and was elected the 40th president of the United States (1981–89). He is remembered for his conservative Republicanism, his fervent anticommunism, and his appealing personal style, characterized by a jaunty affability and folksy charm. The only movie actor ever to become president, he had a remarkable skill as an orator that earned him the title "the Great Communicator." His policies have been credited with contributing to the demise of Soviet communism (Encyclopedia Britannica).

Ronald Reagan presided over some of the most momentous events in the twentieth century and he has garnered the respect and admiration of many. He survived critics and assassins and always seemed to be in the right spot for a good patriotic photograph. Especially among Republicans he is considered one of the greatest Presidents, but he is reviled in other circles and represents the neo-con era's arrival in full force. The love-hate split amongst the public is mostly due to his failed economic policy, which is now known as 'Reaganomics' that ballooned public debt and his secretive foreign policies, such as the Iran-Contra Affair.

Bushes, Clintons, Obamas and Trumps

Americans still live in the era of the neo-con. The politics of its two parties (Republican and Democrat) have become increasingly similar and the transitions between administrations more and more seamless. In America the government has been led by great families for a long time, despite its claims of being representative of the common will of the people. But what if you only have a choice between two candidates? Is that really a choice? When the same people, sometimes related, with the same sorts of agendas appear on the ballot box every election? This seems to have been at least partially responsible for both Barack Obama's back to back terms and then Trump's surprising run for Presidency in 2016. Are Americans fatigued with the establishment politics that have run the country since the Reagan years since the 1980s if not even longer? It seems that it is so.

What is most remarkable about Donald Trump's victory was the haphazard way he seemed to highjack every Republican event on his way to the Presidency, and people claim this was both by design and spontaneous. In Michael Wolf's recent publication *Fire and Fury*, he claims that the Trump campaign did not expect to win and did not in fact want to win! Regardless, it seems clear that a large portion of the public wanted something different, whether it came by popular vote or not. That neither the Democratic governments of Bill Clinton and Barack Obama, nor the Republican governments provided anything substantially different in the way of reform is very telling. The chaos that has ensued should come as no surprise as a leader was elected without a background in politics and without a real vision for a four year term. When everything is said on the spur of the moment, you must expect some things to go awry. This is the current state of the Presidency. Will the contrast be so great that American culture will pivot back to their establishment comfort zone? Will Donald Trump "drain the swamp" and achieve a degree of success? Will the lack of expertise, conflict and investigations bring down the President and the Republicans with him? Or will this experience push the American public's frustration even further and "bring the revolution?" Only time will tell.

Chapter 08

The New World Order

Chapter 08

The New World Order

The Republic & the Two Party System

The Federal Government of the United States is divided into three branches, which were created to provide stability to the state. The concept behind this separation of powers is the system of 'checks and balances.' In creating the three branches it was hoped that when any one branch tried to expand its power or infringe on the jurisdiction of another branch, that a check to its overreach would occur maintaining the balance. The effectiveness of this system is not the object here, as sometimes it has not functioned as intended, but that it has persisted as the model for maintaining the constitution, protecting human rights and preserving democracy in America to this day. Debates have always, and will continue, to swirl around the political manipulations that occur to take advantage or circumvent the principles built into the system, but this is a fundamental aspect of American culture that is constantly referred to by all citizens from the young to the old, the destitute to the obscenely rich. Disillusionment aside, the American system is deeply embedded culturally, financially and socially, thus it is important to look at its structure to gain insight into the experience of being an American, citizen or otherwise.

The Executive Branch is led by an elected President and his proposed Vice-President. The president has the power to veto laws passed through the houses and cause a super majority[1] vote to be required for circumvent the presidential veto. The President as the ability to appoint his own staff and dismiss them. He is Commander in Chief and so holds sway over the American military. She has the power to grant pardons to people who are convicted, without review. When a supreme court justice passes away the President also gets to nominate a new judge for the position.

The Legislative Branch is composed of the House of Representatives and the Senate. There is proportionate representation by state, which is referred to as thr electoral college and those members of a party whose state is won by a party become congressmen and women as a group. Each state elects two senators for a total of 100 members, and they

1 A vote carry two-thirds of the legislative body is required for a super majority

are able to affirm or reject legislation (laws) proposed by the House of Representatives. National budget, new laws, proposals, policies, updates or revisions to Federal Law, all go through both houses before they are submitted to the President to be signed into law.

The Judicial Branch is somewhat unique as its appointed, elected and approved members serve for life. It is the responsibility of the Supreme Court (of which there are 9 members) to hear cases that appeal, refer to, contradict or alter the interpretation of the Constitution. When disputes cannot be resolved politically, or when certain actions have been taken that infringe upon the rights extolled in the Constitution, the Supreme Court must deliberate over matter until they determine whether said action was constitutional or not. Their main role is to render a fair judgment that respects the Constitution and protects Americans.

Of course, it must be reiterated; that is how the American system is supposed to function when the branches act independently of each other. However, corruption, manipulation, partisanship, financial contributions, voter eligibility, lobby groups, public pressure, individual shortcomings and a two party system that forces individuals to follow party lines has made the systems less effective resulting in the current difficulties in American government administration.

Guns

A rifleman takes aim a target in a practice range, which is a common enough practice in many countries, but in America it seems more ominous. Many people maintain that owning a gun, having it loaded and carrying freely are rights that should be protected. However, with the number of "terrorist" acts, which are essentially mass shootings, whether they involve actual plans or are inspired by ideologies or not, have increased in number and deadliness across the United States. Which begs the question: is this a product of American culture? The types of weapons that are involved are not the firearms of the everyday hobbyist, but automatic weapons, sniper rifles and handguns, often with military level equipment and accessories. But again, gun enthusiasts may argue that guns are needed in order to stop other dangerous people with guns, whether they be law enforcement or criminals who are putting people at risk, but the fact remains that among other developed nations these events are much rarer and the results become worse with every new body count. When did it become normal to see only three people dead in a shooting? With every massacre that sets a new record, the number of people required to categorize it as a mass shooting seems to get higher, which is a problem that desperately calls for a solution. American culture is famous for many things, but being dangerous for civilians because of gun violence should not be among them.

The Post 9/11 World

We live in a post 9/11 world.

At 8:46 a.m. on September 11, 2001, a Boeing 767 American Airlines plane flying from Boston to Los Angeles, carrying eighty-one passengers and eleven crew, crashed into the North Tower of the World Trade Center in Manhattan, Seventeen minutes later, another 767m a United Airlines flight carrying fifty-six passengers and nine crew, also en route from Boston to Los Angeles, crashed into the South Tower. At 10:05 the South Tower collapsed, followed, twenty-three minutes later, by the North. In just one hour and forty-two minutes, 2,752 people died. Those who had begun their day with a hurried kiss of farewell, thinking of no more than what they must do and their destinations, found this to be their last day on earth, never knowing why this should be so or that this was, indeed, their fate. After the sudden shock of flame, smoke drifted across the water, papers blew through streets rimed with dust, words unwriting themselves in the artificial night. People stood, unbelieving and yet not altogether unprepared. Figures began to fall, dwarfed by the scale of the buildings, as men and women chose to take their own

> lives rather than have them taken by fire, until the towers themselves fell inwards and down as if consuming themselves. It was, as many remarked, like a dream or a movie and this is why a unique event seemed to stir a sense of déjà vu. For the fact is that the towers had fallen before.[2]

The terrorist attack now known as 9/11 was a singular event in world history and the American government's response to it was predictable. The country quickly went through the stages of grief moving from shock and horror, through guilt, outrage and to anger. Many people knew someone somehow connected to the attack in New York City and the rest of the nation grieved alongside them. In fact, sympathy poured in from all over the world, as the international community closed behind the United States in solidarity, condemning the act and supporting them. However, the desperate need for security and in some measure retaliation produced laws that invaded privacy and infringed on people's rights. It affected citizens, residents and immigrants in profound ways. Freedom was reined in, borders closed, airport security tightened, military spending increased and wars started without sufficient cause. In a country founded on liberty, claiming to be the leader of the free world, this seemed like regression rather than progression. But with the depth of the injury, the terror invoked and the seriousness of the tragedy, the effect was too great not to produce

2 Christopher Bigsby. The Cambridge Companion to Modern American Culture. p. 4.

an equally strong reaction. A revolution of sorts occurred, one based on national security. Policies were changed overnight and a temporary bipartisan consensus formed around President George W. Bush. Emergency measures were declared, troops were mobilized and laws were rushed through the House of Representatives and the Senate. Many of the laws protecting individuals that were earned through the mass protests of the Civil Rights movement in the 1960s were countermanded or replaced. In the post 9/11 era America has become less free and the world continues to deal with the fallout of its domestic and foreign policy decisions as a result of that fateful day.

With by far the most expensive military forces in the world, the United States has the most dominant military in history. No previous nation or state has had the capability of making war anywhere on the planet with so much power. This is the role America has assumed in the Post World War Two era, one which has only one true global superpower.

Thus far the only way to counteract this incredible military dominance has been by developing atomic weapons. Whether a state is an aspiring global superpower, a competitor or a rogue state like North Korea, ostensibly using nuclear weapons as a deterrent, the proliferation of nuclear weapons and states is currently the only real check on the American surface fleet's ability to police the world. Concerns about terrorism aside, the spread of this potentially catastrophic weapons technology has likely been as effective as the American diplomatic and military apparatus itself at maintaining the current state of Pax Americana (American Peace).

The New Millennium

With the ever accelerating pace of technological development and the industrialization of some of the world's oldest and most populous societies, namely China and India, the world has begun its pivot away from Europe and North America and is returning to its ancient focus; Asia. Revolutions have accompanied these changes in China, Japan and Korea. By external and internal pressure, civil war, world war and proxy war, these countries have made dramatic changes to their political systems and their economies have grown exponentially. Other Asian countries are sure to follow in their wake and Africa's awakening may not be in the too distant future either.

The success stories of China, Japan and Korea have been intimately tied to that of the United States, out of necessity and advantage, if not genuine good will. As the leading economic power, the United States formed trade partnerships with East Asia and tapped into their huge human resource pools for labor and production. Likewise, the huge resources and technology of America became available to Asia during the process of globalisation that went into overdrive in the Post World War II era. However, American policy seems to have been frozen in that Cold War environment, and has not adjusted to the incredible changes that have occurred over the last three quarters of a century. Incredible fortunes have been made, amazing technology has been developed, partnerships with people scattered across the globe have formed, but America has been mostly static, allowing the rest of the world to catch up. In fact, in some ways America has devolved, rather than evolved.

Silouettes of army personnel demonstrate the stereotypes and biases we have about militarism. Despite it being "the land of the free," America is also the "home of the brave." If you were to color in these shadows with camouflage, paint, faces and flags. Which country do you imagine doing these drills, moving to these positions, firing these weapons and operating this equipment? Most often, you would answer: America.

America's economic power as a proportion of global GDP peaked in the mid-20th century, its military leadership became less relevant once the Cold War had run its course, its public debt has ballooned to epic proportions, its negative trade balance with the aforementioned East Asian countries has exploded, its middle class has lost the income equality and financial security in had in the decades after World War II, the civil rights and freedom earned in the 1960s protests have been gradually rolled back and its ability for political consensus and bipartisanship beyond preserving the power of the elite has all but disappeared as its two political parties are at constant loggerheads.

In many respects the golden age of America, both domestically and internationally, has passed.

So if that is the case, that the evolution of the culture and state is at an impasse, what is required to get it going again? Many Americans have become increasingly desperate in their quest to answer this question. They have pushed for reform, but their politicians have been unwilling or unable to follow through. This was one of the major factors in Donald Trump's 2016 campaign leading to his election to the Presidential office over Hillary Clinton. Americans went to the polls and narrowly decided in favor of Trump, a political outsider who high-jacked the Republican Party convention, over Clinton a seasoned establishment democrat. The desire to break the status quo, even if it meant voting for a politically unproven and untested candidate, seems implicit in the results. Needless to say the outcome has not been a drastic improvement over previous presidents and the administrations of the past several decades. The United States Government is rapidly losing the respect and the trust it has earned around the world over the past hundred years, but to some the instability that has come with an administration that seems at odds with itself and many of the world's most influential leaders and nations may finally be the thing to break the deadlock. In the words of a young African-American woman speaking out on the campaign trail: "... I don't like Trump! I'm just gonna vote for him because he'll bring the Revolution."

Not unlike this young woman, people have been preaching, teachers have been teaching, students have been protesting, authors have been writing, and artists have been performing; trying to drive the social and cultural revolution that some think is on the horizon. Many forms of art have expressed this idea over the years, but perhaps the most energetic and closely tied to the current generation is music. Just as pamphlets and paintings, magazines, manifestos and speeches have driven countercultures toward revolution in the past, songs have their place today, and the list of songs and their powerful lyrics are as plentiful as they are myriad. Here are two influential songs to take as representative samples mirroring some of cultural movement and revolutionary spirit that has been described in the pages of this book; the first American, the second British:

Rage Against the Machine

Sleep Now in the Fire from the album The Battle of Los Angeles

Songwriters: Brad J. Wilk / Thomas B. Morello / Timothy Commerford / Zack M. De La Rocha

The world is my expense
The cost of my desire
Jesus blessed me with its future
And I protect it with fire

So raise your fists

And march around

Don't dare take what you need

I'll jail and bury those committed

And smother the rest in greed

Crawl with me into tomorrow

Or I'll drag you to your grave

I'm deep inside your children

They'll betray you in my name

Sleep now in the fire

The lie is my expense

The scope of my desire

The Party blessed me with its future

And I protect it with fire

I am the Nina ThePinta The Santa Maria

The noose and the rapist

And the fields overseer

The agents of orange

The priests of Hiroshima

The cost of my desire

Sleep now in the fire

For it's the end of history

It's caged and frozen still

There is no other pill to take

So swallow the one

That made you ill

The Nina The Pinta The Santa Maria

The noose and the rapist

The fields overseer

The agents of orange

The priests of Hiroshima

The cost of my desire

Sleep now in the fire

Degeneration

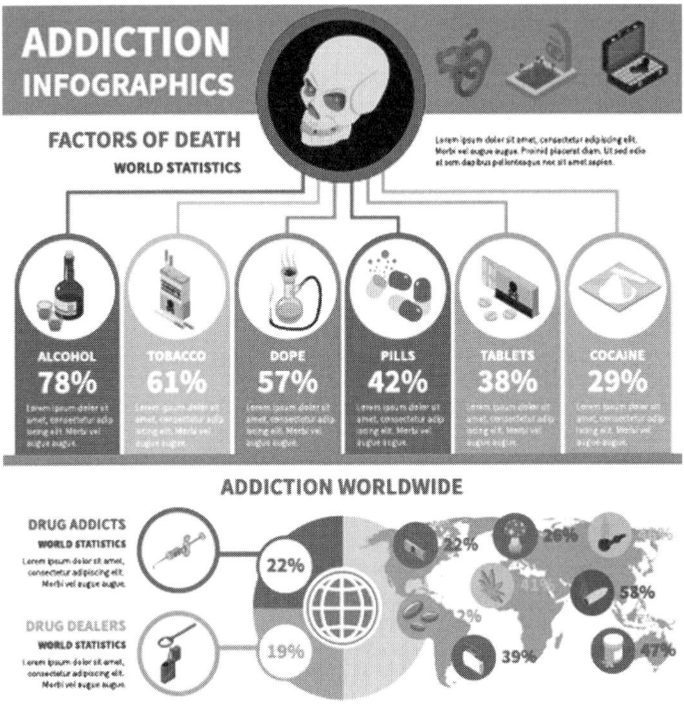

Is American culture devolving and degenerating? Has British culture settled into a resigned century long lull and a backseat in global influence? Both societies still have great strengths, but they cannot help but be compared to their past heights. Looking at the next generation and their cultural heritage offers some insight into these questions.

Increasingly the youth of developed countries have been lured by drugs that are produced internationally and despite its official anti-drug stance, the existence of the D.E.A. and billions of dollars spent on the "War on Drugs," this is not a war that America is winning.

Americans spend more money on drugs than any people on earth and British people are some of the highest per capita consumers. This may sound scary to many, but it is worth asking, 'why are so many people taking drugs?' Is it social pressure, depression, profit, culture or other factors? Furthermore, is there even anything fundamentally wrong with the consumption of drugs? Alcohol is both the most common and the most lethal drug by total numbers in the world, if one does not count secondary death by disease like lung cancer or heart attacks and the other most commonly consumed and legalized drug would be: tobacco. Does America have a drug problem? Is it related to its cultural problems? Is the United Kingdom in the same boat? Again, these are questions that few people have answers for, but they are questions that should be addressed going forward considering the harm done to society and the number of individuals in prison for relatively minor drug related offences. Both seem indicative of some underlying social and cultural inconsistencies. The following rap lyrics by Asian Dub Foundation are copied below (listening along to the song is recommended to get a feel for the "real Great Britain") which may provide some insight into a cultural perspective on the state of the British. It is not drug-fueled or even drug-related, but one gets that sense that national identity and cultural norms are intimately caught up in both. The sense of being trapped in a society: "forever looking backward."

Asian Dub Foundation

The Real Great Britain from the album *Community Music*

Written by: Das, Pandit, Savale, Tailor and Zaman

http://asiandubfoundation.com/site/

Union jack and union jill
Back up and down the same old hill
Sell the flag to the youths
But who swallows the bill
"Murdoch she wrote"
Him have his hand in the till

Blairful of Thatcher
Stuck on the 45
The suits have changed
But the old ties survive
New Britannia cool
Who are you trying to fool?
Behind your fashion-tashion I see nothing at all

Care for the commodity
Cuts the nation into three
Rich pickings for the first

Bottom third you never see
While middle England keeps swinging its
Loyalty
No concern for the future
Just with dead royalty

So will the real, the real great britain
Step forward
This is the national identity parade
Shoe gazer nation forever looking
Backwards
Time to reject the sixties charade

Not enough schools
Not enough homes
Just "phony care" in his millennium dome
More prime cuts than beef on the bone
And there's too many questions you're
Not answering tone

Union jack and union jill
Back up and down the same old hill
Sell the flag to the youths
But who swallows the bill

"Murdoch she wrote"
Him have his hand in the till

So will the real, the real Great Britain
Step forward
This is the national identity parade
Shoe gazer nation forever looking
Backwards
Time to reject the sixties charade

Conclusion

Conclusion

Determining how to conclude a broad work on culture such as this has dogged the whole writing process as a traditional conclusion may not be a good fit here. The evolution of these cultures is ongoing and so this topic remains open. Nonetheless, I would like to leave the reader with a message and some possible applications for the information contained herein. Howard Zinn reflects on the monumental task of constructing a book of history whether it encompasses an entire culture, nation or history or just a part:

> By the time I began teaching and writing, I had no illusions about "objectivity," If that meant avoiding a point of view. I knew that a

historian (or a journalist, or anyone telling a story) was forced to choose, out of an infinite number of facts, what to present, what to omit. And that decision inevitably would reflect, whether consciously or not, the interests of the historian.

There is a certain drumbeat of scolding one hears these days, about the need for students to learn facts. "Our young people are not being taught facts," said Presidential candidate Robert Dole (and candidates are always scrupulous about facts) to a gathering of American Legionnaires. I was reminded of the character in Dickens' Hard Times, the pedant Gradgrind, who admonished a younger teacher: "Teach nothing but facts, facts, facts."[1]

My project has rejected that assumption, just as Howard Zinn did in A People's History of the United States; that we should only speak of facts and teach them. We must rely on them and dig for the facts and use them in trying to understand what happened and who we are and who we should be. Without the proper knowledge to begin with we could not proceed, but it is our responsibility to go beyond the facts and discover what they mean, not just what they are. Which is why it is so important to remember that, "...there is no such thing as pure fact, innocent of interpretation. Behind every fact presented to the world—by a teacher, a writer, anyone—is a judgment. The judgment that has been made is that this fact is important, and the other facts, omitted, are not important."[2]

Writing in Korea while having a background in British and American Literature and being raised in Canada has given a certain flavor to this account of British and American culture that is undeniable. Presenting

1 Howard Zinn. A People's History of the United States. P. 683-684

2 Howard Zinn. A People's History of the United States. P. 684

the facts and leading the reader on a whirlwind tour through certain perspectives on certain components of this incredibly complex subject has been the goal and now it has run its course. This is just a base from which to launch yourself into the contemplation, understanding, application and active engagement with the culture that you choose. It is our duty to continue the quest to understand all cultures, not just British and American, going forward. This makes us better citizens. In closing the following poem by Lord Alfred Tennyson, *Oh Ye We Trust*, is written below. Not to leave behind any religious message, but to recall the common experiences of all human beings and the evolution of human culture:

Oh Yet We Trust

Oh yet we trust that somehow good
Will be the final goal of ill,
To pangs of nature, sins of will,
Defects of doubt, and taints of blood;

That nothing walks with aimless feet;
That not one life shall be destroyed,
Or cast as rubbish to the void,
When God hath made the pile complete;

That not a worm is cloven in vain;
That not a moth with vain desire

Is shrivelled in a fruitless fire,
Or but subserves another's gain.

Behold, we know not anything;
I can but trust that good shall fall
At last—far off—at last, to all,
And every winter change to spring.

So runs my dream: but what am I?
An infant crying in the night:
An infant crying for the light:
And with no language but a cry.[3]

3 Lord Alfred Tennyson. Immortal Poems of the English Language.p. 391.

British and American Culture:
Evolution and Revolution

Appendix

Appendix

Appendix I
The Principal Wars of England and Great Britain

As we discussed earlier in the book, Great Britain is really only a part of the United Kingdom of Great Britain and Northern Ireland, but it is of course, the largest part. Great Britain itself is an island off the northwest coast of Europe and which was once referred to as the Atlantic isles by Europeans and is comprised of three countries: England, Scotland, and Wales.

The important battles and wars in British history are innumerable. In fact only the most significant of engagements have been recorded and of those most people only know a handful of the most famous victories and infamous defeats. Military history has underpinned much of this book, but instead of being bogged down with the detailing of each conflict as the history of British culture unfolded, it will be summarized here, for the reader's reference. With the briefest of summaries, and with many notable omissions the list starts below with the Norman Conquest and ends in the present day:

The Norman Conquest of England (1066-1072) - The Battle of Hastings was the climactic moment of this "war," which really only amounted to a season of fighting followed by the armed suppression of English baron led peasant revolts. King Harold was defeated by William the Conqueror in the fall of 1066 after racing north to crush an invading Viking force and then dashing back to meet Duke William at Hastings, blocking the way to London. The Normans defeated the Anglo-Saxon (English) army, killed Harold and took the capital. They spread across Angle-land and even crossed over to Ireland to collect more territory and spoils. The harsh Norman rule that spread to the border of the Scots is commonly known as the "Harrowing of the North." King William's response was to burn, execute and massacre those associated with the armed resistance in York and Northumbria eventually stamping out any remaining Anglo-Saxon presence with brute force.

The Hundred Years' War (1337-1453) - The Hundred Years' War was not actually a single war but long periods of occupation and invasion which were broken up by treaties that temporarily halted the bloodshed. England was fighting for its ancestral rights to territories in northern France and the king was trying to assert his hereditary right to the throne. The entire war between France lasted 116 years. It featured some of the most well-known battles and historical figures of the period that became legends after their time. Most historians break this conflict into four distinct wars.

The War of the Roses (1455-1485) - This was perhaps the most infamous of England's wars until the Civil War displaced it. After all the drama (that has been immortalized in Shakespeare's historical plays and again by George R.R. Martin, the House of Lancaster (a.ka. the Tudor family) defeated the House of York.

The English Civil War (1641-1651) - This was actually three related civil conflicts between the English Parliament and its supporters against the Royalist followers of King Charles I and King Charles II. The first was called the Bishop's War as the English tried to impose the Anglican book of prayer on the Scots, and the second and third are just known as the first and second civil wars, just to confuse the amateur historian. The war resulted in the temporary overthrow of the English monarchy.

The First Anglo-Dutch War (1652-1654) - This war was fought primarily at sea and was a struggle for maritime dominance between the two rival Protestant states. Both sides lost ships, men and trade so the war was ended.

The Second Anglo-Dutch War (1664-1667) - War was rekindled between the Netherlands and England when they were unable to share the high seas and their lucrative trade monopolies.

The Third Anglo-Dutch War (1672-1674) - A third and final war was fought between the two states with the English gaining the upper hand. As a consequence of these conflicts the

The War of the Quadruple Alliance (1718-1720) - This war involved Great Britain, the Holy Roman Empire, France, the Dutch Republic, and Sardinia being allied against the Kingdoms of Spain.

The War of the Austrian Succession (1742-1748) - Great Britain, Austria and Holland went to war against France and Prussia over the Habsburg dynasty's possession of Holy Roman territories.

King George's War (1744-1748) - The North American portion of this war, fought between Britain and France in their American colonies.

The Seven Years' War (1756-1763) - In what has been called the "first truly global war" the allied states of Great Britain and Prussia fought against Austria, France, Russia, Sweden, and Spain. The British forces were primarily engaged with the French on the sea, in Europe, Asia and North America.

The French and Indian War (1754-1763) - The North American theater of the Seven Years' war, which was fought between Britain and France in their American colony with the aid of the Native American allies. The conflict ended decisively on the plains of Abraham with General Wolfe's victory over Montcalme at the battle of Quebec. The French ultimately surrendered the territory of Nouvelle France (New

France) to the British in the Treaty of Paris.

The American War of Independence (1775-1783) - This war was fought between the generals of the British Empire, principally led by Sir Thomas Gage and then "the triumvirate of reputation" Major general Howe and Brigadiers general John Burgoyne and Henry Clinton. With the tenacious and charismatic General George Washington commanding the continental forces it became only a matter of time before the British bungled away early their advantages. The conflict officially ended with the Second Treaty of Paris in 1783, recognizing the sovereignty of the United States of America.

The War of the First Coalition (1792-1798) - Britain, Austria, Prussia, Spain, Russia, Sardinia and the Low Countries formed an alliance in order to combat Revolutionary France. Russia left the Coalition in 1794 as it had domestic issues to deal with in its empires as the Polish revolted. French victories forced the Low Countries (then known as the Austrian Netherlands and later remade as the Batavian Republic by occupying French forces), to leave the Coalition in 1795. Prussia and Spain made a separate peace with the French in 1795 and Austria signed the Treaty of Campo-Formio in 1798 after getting soundly beaten by a certain revolutionary general pulling off stunning victories in the Austrian occupied Italian states, Napoleon Bonaparte. In that treaty the Austrians surrendered the territory that roughly conforms to Belgium and the Netherlands to France.

The War of the Second Coalition (1798-1801) - Great Britain,

Austria, Russia, Portugal, Naples and the Ottoman Empire combined to fight Revolutionary France. Spain later joined France against Portugal. This alliance against France formed to counter French moves in Italy; formation of the Roman, Ligurian, Cisalpine and Helvetic Republics in Switzerland and Italy, and the deposition of Papal rule in Rome. Naples was conquered by the French in early 1799 and declared to be the new Parthenopean Republic. Napoleon Bonaparte invaded Turkish Egypt and won the Battle of the Pyramids, continuing his march into what is now Israel and Lebanon. British Admiral Horatio Nelson wiped out the French fleet at the Battle of the Nile in 1798. Due to French victories on land against both Turkish and British troops, the Ottoman Empire made peace with France at the Convention of El-Arish in 1800.

The Anglo-French War (1803-1814) - While other European nations waged war and then sued for peace against Napoleonic France, Britain was in a continual state of war against France from 1803 through the first defeat of Napoleon in 1814.

The Peninsular War (1807-1814) - This war began with the French Invasions of Portugal and Spain, and was fought in parallel with other wars on other fronts. Great Britainsent expeditionary forces to help the Portuguese and Spanish drive out the French. From the British perspective, the Peninsular War was a part of the long-running war between Britain and France from 1803 to 1814.

The War of 1812 (1812-1814) - The second war between the United

States and Great Britain fought principally in the North American theater between British North America, which would become the Dominion of Canada in 1867, and the United States.

The War of the Seventh Coalition (1815) - After Napoleon's return to France from exile, Britain, Russia, Prussia, Sweden, Austria, the Netherlands and a number of smaller German states combined to fight Napoleon and France. The allies defeated Napoleon once and for all at the Battle of Waterloo.

The First Opium War (1839-1842) - This war, conducted in mainland China, had a variety of causes, but most important to the British was the Chinese reluctance to open their ports to international trade. Leading up to the conflict was the British insistence on selling Opium, which millions of Chinese became addicted to, in exchange for valuable products and commodities that could be sold for large profit in the European market.

The Crimean War (1853-1856) - Britain, France, and Sardinia joined together to aid the Ottoman Empire, which was under attack by Russia.

The Second Opium War (1856-1860) - British-Chinese War when the Chinese Empire again resisted western efforts to maintain trade with its ports and secure more trade concessions

The First Boer War (1880-1881) - This war was fought between the British forces and the Boers who were or Dutch-descent in areas in Africa around what is now the country of South Africa.

The Second Boer War (1899-1902) - Britain vs. The Boer Republics (Orange Free State and Transvaal) in what is now South Africa.

The Boxer Rebellion (1899-1900) - The Chinese secret religious and nationalistic Society of the Righteous Harmonious Fists (Boxers), initiated a rebellion against both foreign colonizers, missionaries and their own government in 1899. By 1900, the Chinese government had co-opted the rebels and directed their violent fury entirely upon the foreign presence in China. The Boxers, aided by Chinese Imperial troops, besieged the diplomatic legations (embassies) of the Western powers and Japan, sparking a truly international response. A retaliatory relief expedition composed of troops from: the United State, Great Britain, France, Germany, Italy, Austria-Hungary, Russia and Japan invaded China and captured the capital of Peking (now called Beijing).

World War One (1914-1918) - This is considered the first "official" world war and was originally known as "The Great War," and also as "The World War."

The Russian Civil War - Britain, along with the United States, France, and Japan, intervened unsuccessfully in the civil war in Russia that brought the Communists to power.

The Anglo-Irish War (1919-1921) - Resulted in the formation of the Irish Free State, and the division of Ireland, with the six northern counties (Ulster), chosing to remain a part of the United Kingdom.

World War Two (1939-1945) - This war may be the most difficult of all to describe. At one point in 1940 it was Hitler's Nazi regime vs.

Great Britain making for a very lopsided match on paper. However, there was one thing preventing Germany's conquest of the United Kingdom, the channel. As always, that barrier needed to be overcome, and that meant defeating the British fleet. In order to defeat the British fleet the Germans needed to gain air superiority, thus began the Battle of Britain and the "London Blitz." However, the British endured the bombing and fought for control of the air and the Luftwaffe was unable to complete their mission. Thus, just like Napoleon, Hitler turned his eyes toward the Eastern front and sent his armies into Russia alleviating the pressure on the British. Sir Winston Churchill continued the resistance until the Americans joined the war and the allies gradually retook territory from the Nazis resulting in an allied victory complete surrender of European Axis forces in 1945.

The Cold War (1945-1990) - The United Kingdom of GreatBritain, along with its allies in NAFTA, predominantly the United States, fought proxy wars representing capitalism against the Russian and Chinese dominated Communist nations of Asia and their allies in the eastern block of European nations. In 1946 Winston Churchill described the division of European nations in a famous speech saying, "From Stettin in the Baltic to Trieste in the Adriatic, an iron curtain has descended across the continent."

The Greek Civil War (1944-1947) - British forces became involved in the early stages of the Greek Civil War when they liberated Greece from German occupation toward the end of 1944. As the Germans withdrew, competing Greek factions fought for control. The British sided with the re-established Greek government against the Communist rebels. Due to financial pressures and their own need to recover from World War Two, Britain announced a withdrawal of forces in 1947. The Greek Civil War continued until 1949, with the United States taking over the role of protector for the government. British combat involvement primarily took place in 1944 and 1945. The Greek Civil War continued until the Greek government defeated the rebels in 1949.

The Korean War (1950-1953) - When the Cold War suddenly became hot the United Nations was called upon to intervene on the behave of the beleaguered South Korean Forces assisting the American military in repelling the North Korean forces and then preventing the Chinese army from advancing down the peninsula. Great Britain provided the second most soldiers after the United States, with the former British states of Canada and Australia supplying the third and fifth most troops (Turkey sent the fourth most).

Anglo-Egyptian War (1951-1952) - Egyptian guerrillas, aided by the governement carried out a campaign against British forces stationed at the Suez Canal and agains other symbols of Britain and the West. On January 25, 1952, British troops retaliated against Egypt by attacking an Egyptian police station, killing 50 and wounding 100. The conflict ended with a change in the Egyptian government and the eventual withdrawal of British troops. This conflict led to Britain's involvement in the 1956 Anglo-French-Israeli invasion of Egypt in 1956.

The Suez War (1956-1956) - Britain and France invaded Egypt (in conjunction with Israel), in an ill-planned attempt to take control of the Suez Canal from Egypt.

Muscat and Oman Intervention (1957-1959) - In this conflict British troops supported the government of Muscat and Oman (now known simply as Oman), against rebels. British troops withdrew after a successful campaign.

The Jordan Intervention (1958) - Britain airlifted troops to Jordan in response to a request for aid from the Jordanian king. King Hussein felt threatened by the recent union of Syria and Egypt, as well as the violent revolution in Iraq in which the Iraq king, a member of Hussein's family, was brutally murdered. After the situation calmed down, British troops left Jordan.

The Falkland Islands War (1982) - The military dictatorship in Argentina mistakenly believed that Britain, led by Prime Minister Margaret "Iron Lady" Thatcher, would not wage a war over the tiny Falkland Islands in the South Atlantic. When the Argentines invaded the British-owned and British-inhabited Falkland Islands in April of 1982, the British responded by sending the Royal Navy and other military units to liberate the islands from the Argentine invaders. The British defeated the Argentines and liberated the islands. As a direct result of the disasterous war with Britain, the Argentine dictatorship fell and was replaced by a democracy.

The Gulf War (1991) - The United Kingdom was one of the United States main allies in its retaliatory action against the Iraqi invasion of Kuwait. As a consequence of the difference in weapons technology the Iraqi army was defeated and its remnants were harried back into Iraqi territory in a matter of days. The allied attack was codenamed operation Desert Storm.

The Bosnian War (1995–1996) - This was a joint NATO operation to protect Bosnia from Bosnian Serb rebels and regular Serbian military forces.

The Kosovo War (1999) - This was a joint NATO operation to protect Kosovar Muslims from Serbian militias and regular Serbian military forces.

Afghanistan War (2001-Present) - Britain joined with the United States and other allies to oust the Taliban and al-Qaida from power in Afghanistan in the wake of al-Qaida's September 11 attacks on the United States.

The Iraq War (2003-2009) - Britain, along with the U.S., Australia, and Poland, invaded Iraq to drive out the regime of Dictator Saddam Hussein.British forces ended their participation in the war in Iraq on April 30, 2009.

The Libyan War (2011) - The UK joined with other NATO nations and pro-Western Sunni Arab nations to aid Libyan rebels overthrow Libyan dictator Muammar Ghaddaffi.

Appendix II.

Principal Wars or Conflicts in Which the United States Participated: U.S. Military Personnel Serving and Casualties (1775-1991)

			Casualties			
War or Conflict	Branch of Service	Number Serving	Total Deaths	Battle Deaths	Other Deaths	Wounds Not Mortala
Revolutionary War[b] 1775-1783	**Total**	**—**	**4,435**	**4,435**	**—**	**6,188**
	Army	—	4,044	4,044	—	6,004
	Navy	—	342	342	—	114
	Marines	—	49	49	—	70
War of 1812[c] 1812-1815	**Total**	**286,730**	**2,260**	**2,260**	**—**	**4,505**
	Army	—	1,950	1,950	—	4,000
	Navy	—	265	265	—	439
	Marines	—	45	45	—	66
Mexican War[c] 1846-1848	**Total**	**78,718**	**13,283**	**1,733**	**11,550**	**4,152**
	Army	—	13,271	1,721	11,550	4,102
	Navy	—	1	1	—	3
	Marines	—	11	11	—	47
Civil War[cd] (Union Forces Only)[e] 1861-1865	**Total**	**2,213,363**	**364,511**	**140,414**	**224,097**	**281,881**
	Army	2,128,948	359,528	138,154	221,374	280,040
	Navy	84,415	4,523	2,112	2,411	1,710

	Marines	f	460	148	312	131
Spanish-American War 1898-1901	**Total**	**306,760**	**2,446**	**385**	**2,061**	**1,662**
	Army[g]	280,564	2,430	369	2,061	1,594
	Navy	22,875	10	10	—	47
	Marines	3,321	6	6	—	21
World War I 1917-1918	**Total**	**4,734,991**	**116,516**	**53,402**	**63,114**	**204,002**
	Army[h]	4,057,101	106,378	50,510	55,868	193,663
	Navy	599,051	7,287	431	6,856	819
	Marines	78,839	2,851	2,461	390	9,520
World War II[i] 1941-1946[j]	**Total**	**16,112,566**	**405,399**	**291,557**	**113,842**	**670,846**
	Army[k]	11,260,000	318,274	234,874	83,400	565,861
	Navy[l]	4,183,466	62,614	36,950	25,664	37,778
	Marines	669,100	24,511	19,733	4,778	67,207
Korean War[m] 1950-1953	**Total**	**5,720,000**	**36,574**	**33,739**	**2,835**	**103,284**
	Army	2,834,000	29,856	27,731	2,125	77,596
	Navy	1,177,000	657	503	154	1,576
	Marines	424,000	4,509	4,267	242	23,744
	Air Force	1,285,000	1,552	1,238	314	368
Vietnam Conflict[n] 1964-1973	**Total**	**8,744,000**	**58,220**	**47,434**	**10,786**	**Hosp. Care Req'd: 153,303 No Hospital Care: 150,341**

	Army	4,368,000	38,224	30,963	7,261	Hosp. Care Req'd: 96,802 No Hospital Care: 104,723
	Navy	1,842,000	2,566	1,631	935	Hosp. Care Req'd: 4,178 No Hospital Care: 5,898
	Marines	794,000	14,844	13,095	1,749	Hosp. Care Req'd: 51,392 No Hospital Care: 37,202
	Air Force	1,740,000	2,586	1,745	841	Hosp. Care Req'd: 931 No Hospital Care: 2,518
Persian Gulf War 1990-1991	**Total**	**2,225,000**	**383**	**148**	**235**	**467**
	Army	782,000	224	98	126	354
	Navy	669,000	56	6	50	12
	Marines	213,000	68	24	44	92
	Air Force	561,000	35	20	15	9

Source: Defense Casualty Analysis System (DCAS), https://www.dmdc.osd.mil/dcas/pages/report_principal_wars.xhtml.

Notes: Data prior to World War I are based on incomplete records in many cases. Casualty data are confined to dead and wounded and, therefore, exclude personnel captured or missing in action who were subsequently returned to military control.

a. Marine Corps data for World War II, the Spanish-American War, and prior wars represent the number of individuals wounded, whereas all other data in this column represent the total number (incidence) of wounds.

b. Number serving not known, but estimates range from 184,000 to 250,000.

c. As reported by the Commissioner of Pensions in the annual report for FY1903.

d. The Civil War (1861-1865) produced the most American casualties, when both Union statistics and Confederate estimates are taken into account.

e. Authoritative statistics for the Confederate forces are not available. Estimates of the number who served range from 600,000 to 1,500,000. The final report of the Provost Marshal General, 1863-1866, indicated 133,821 Confederate deaths (74,524 battle and 59,297 other) based upon incomplete returns. In addition, an estimated 26,000 to 31,000 Confederate personnel died in Union prisons.

f. The Marine Corps number serving is included in the Navy total.

g. Number serving covers the period April 21, 1898, to August 13, 1898, whereas dead and wounded data are for the period May 1, 1898, to August 31, 1898. Active hostilities ceased on August 13, 1898, but ratifications of the Treaty of Peace were not exchanged between the United States and Spain until April 11, 1899.

h. Includes air service. Battle deaths and wounds not mortal include casualties suffered by American forces in northern Russia to August 25, 1919, and in Siberia to April 1, 1920. Other deaths cover the period from April 1, 1917, to December 31, 1918.

i. World War II was the first war in which there were more American battle casualties than deaths from other causes, such as accidents, disease, and infections.

j. Data are for the period December 1, 1941, through December 31, 1946, when hostilities were officially terminated by presidential proclamation, but a few battle deaths or wounds not mortal were incurred after the Japanese acceptance of the Allied peace terms on August 14, 1945. Numbers serving from December 1, 1941, through August 31, 1945, were as follows: Total 14,903,213; Army 10,420,000; Navy 3,883,520; and Marine Corps 599,693.

k. Includes Army air forces, also known as the Army Air Corps.

l. Battle deaths and wounds not mortal include casualties incurred in October 1941 due to hostile

British and American Culture:
Evolution and Revolution

Bibliography

Bibliography

Austen, Jane. *Pride and Prejudice*. London: Penguin Books, 2003.

Bigsby, Christopher, Ed. *The Cambridge Companion to Modern American Culture*. Cambridge, UK: Cambridge University Press, 2006.

Catton, Bruce. *The Civil War*. New York, NY: Mariner Books, 2004.

Diamond, Jared. *Guns, Germs and Steel: The Fates of Human Societies*. New York, NY: W.W. Norton & Company, 1999.

EnclopediaBritannica. https://www.britannica.com. Date accessed: November 1, 2017-February 4, 2018.

Fraser, Rebecca. *The Story of Britain: From the Romans to the Present: A Narrative History*. New York: NY. W.W. Norton & Company, 2003.

Gilliam, Terry, et al. *Monty Python and the Holy Grail*.Columbia Tristar Home Entertainment, 2002.

Hartman, Andrew. *A War for the Soul of America: A History of the Culture Wars*. Chicago: University of Chicago Press, 2015.

Herman, Arthur. *How the Scots Invented the Modern World: The True Story of How Western Europe's Poorest Nation Created Our World & Everything in It.* New York, NY: Random House, 2001.

Herman, Arthur. To Rule the Waves: How the British Navy Shaped the Modern World. New York, NY: HarperCollins, 2004.

Higgins, Michael, Clarissa Smith and John Storey, Ed.*The Cambridge Companion to Modern British Culture*. Cambridge, UK: Cambridge University Press 2010.

Izzard, Eddie. *Dressed to Kill.* Orpheum Theatre, San Francisco, California: Video Vision, 1998. Live.

James, Lawrence. *The Rise & Fall of the British Empire*. London, UK: Little, Brown Book Group, 1998.

Lacey, Robert.*Great Tales from English History*. New York, NY: Back Bay Books, 2007.

Lasn, Kalle. *Culture Jam: How to Reverse America's Suicidal Consumer Binge—and Why We Must*. New York, NY: HarperCollins, 2000.

Herbert, Lawrence D H (David. Women in Love. Random House, 1950.

Lawson, M. K. Cnut: England's Viking King. Stroud, Ireland. History Press, 2011.

Loewen, James W. *Lies My Teacher Told Me: Everything Your American History Textbook Got Wrong*. New York, NY: Touchstone, 2007.

Lugton, Robert C. *American Topics: A Reading Voculary Text for Speakers of English as a Second Language*. 2nd Ed. Englewood Cliffs, New Jersey: Prentice-Hall, 1986.

Merullo, Annabel and Neil Wenborn, Ed. *British Military Greats*. London, UK: Cassell Illustrated, 2004.

O'Shaughnessy, Andrew Jackson. *The Men Who Lost America: British Leadership, the American Revolution, and the Fate of the Empire*. New Haven, CT: Yale University Press, 2013.

Schweikart, Larry and Marcus Allen.*A Patriot's History of the United States: From Columbus's Great Discovery to America's Age of Entitlement*. New York, NY: Sentinel, 2014.

Shakespeare, William, and Charles R. Forker. *King Richard II*. London: Arden Shakespeare, 2002. Print.

Sir Gawain and the Green Knight. Trans. Brian Stone. London: Penguin Books, 2nd ed., 1974.

Smith, A. *The Harvard Classics 10: An Inquiry into the Nature and Causes of the Wealth of Nations*. C. W. Eliot, Ed. New York: P. F. Collier & Son, 1909. Print.

Smith, Lacey Baldwin. *English History Made Brief, Irreverent, and Pleasurable*. Chicago, Illinois: Academy Chicago Publishers, 2007.

Shakespeare, William, and G. R. Hibbard. *Hamlet*. Oxford University Press, 2008.

Stoute, Steve. *The Tanning of America*. New York: Penguin Books, 2011.

Swift, Jonathan. *Gulliver's Travels and "A Modest Proposal."* New York: Pocket Books, 2005.

Tennyson, Lord Alfred. "Oh Yet We Trust." Immortal Poems of the English Language.Ed. Oscar Williams. New York: Washing Square Press, 1952. 391.

Tocqueville, Alexis de, and Isaac Kramnick. Trans. Gerald E. Bevan. *Democracy in America and Two Essays on America*. London: Penguin Books, 2003.

Toombs, Robert. *The English and Their History*. New York, NY: Vintage Books, 2014.

Twain, Mark. *Adventures of Huckleberry Finn*. New York, NY: Signet Classics, 1997.

Woodward, Colin. *American Nations: A History of the Eleven Rival Regional Cultures of North America*. New York, NY: Penguin Group, 2012.

Woolf, Virginia. Mrs Dalloway. Penguin, 1996.

Wordsworth, William. Lyrical Ballads. Routledge, 2013.

Zinn, Howard. A People's History of the United States. New York, NY: HarperCollins, 2003.

American History in 50 Events. Middletown, DE: Hourly History, 2015.

"Defense Casualty Analysis System (DCAS)."*DMDC*.https://www.dmdc.osd.mil/dcas/pages/report_principal_wars.xhtml.Web. Date Accessed:December 12, 2017.

Nationmaster.http://www.nationmaster.com/country-info/stats/Agriculture/Arable-land/Hectares. Web. Date Accessed: January 21, 2018.

Illustration Credits

https://modis.gsfc.nasa.gov/gallery/individual.php?db_date=2012-06-04

http://etc.usf.edu/clipart/45200/45225/45225_britain_arms_lg.gif

https://media1.britannica.com/eb-media/74/94574-004-F81E504A.jpg

http://www.emersonkent.com/images/maps/native_american_map.jpg